New Business Matters

Workbook

business English with a lexical approach

Charles Mercer

THOMSON

HEINLE

United Kingdom • United States • Australia • Canada • Mexico • Singapore • Spain

New Business Matters
Workbook
Charles Mercer

Publisher: *Chris Wenger*
Director of Editorial Development: *Anita Raducanu*
Director of Marketing: *Amy Mabley*
Editorial Manager: *Howard Middle/HM ELT Services*
Development Editor: *Jean Pender*
Sr. Production Editor: *Sally Cogliano*
Sr. Print Buyer: *Mary Beth Hennebury*
Associate Marketing Manager: *Laura Needham*

Compositor: *Process ELT (www.process-elt.com)*
Production Management: *Process ELT*
Photography Manager: *Sheri Blaney*
Photo Researcher: *Loukas Ioannou, Process ELT*
Copyeditor: *Katerina Mestheneou*
Cover/Text Designer: *Studio Image & Photographic Art*
(www.studio-image.com)
Printer: *Seng Lee Press*

Printed in Singapore.
1 2 3 4 5 6 7 8 9 10 07 06 05 04 03

For more information contact Thomson Learning, High Holborn House 50/51 Bedford Row, London WC1R 4LR United Kingdom or Heinle, 25 Thomson Place, Boston, Massachusetts 02210 USA. You can visit our Web site at http://www.heinle.com

For permission to use material from this text or product, submit a request online at www.thomsonrights.com

ISBN: 0-7593-9859-3
(Workbook)

Contents

To the student

This Workbook accompanies the New Business Matters Coursebook and is intended to i) revise and explain key grammar points, ii) help you to revise and practise business English expressions and learn new vocabulary and iii) develop both your reading and writing skills for business.

Each four-page unit follows the theme of the Coursebook unit it practises, and consists of one or two Language Focus sections, followed by Language Development, and Writing.

Language Focus

Each unit begins with one or sometimes two Language Focus sections which revise essential grammar and provide a framework for accuracy in your spoken and written business English. The Language Focus pages not only concentrate on basic grammar structures, but also give you the chance to practise these structures as well as use the vocabulary you have learnt in the Coursebook. At the same time, new vocabulary is also introduced.

Language Development

In addition, each unit offers a Language Development page where you will be able to test and expand your knowledge drawn from the Coursebook. This section not only recycles vocabulary used in the Coursebook, but also adds synonyms and introduces new words. In this way, by carefully following the exercises in both books, you will be able to expand your business English vocabulary.

Writing

Although electronic communication has influenced English in recent years and made it more informal, especially in e-mails, there is still a requirement to produce language written in a formal register for business. By referring to the Model Answer section on pages 73-75 you will find examples of correspondence used in business communications. The language used in each example reflects the standard of formality expected by companies who conduct their day-to-day business in English.

BEC Vantage Examination

The Business English Certificates (BEC) Vantage Examination

If you wish to use this book to help you pass the Cambridge BEC Vantage exam, you will find many of the exercises have been set, within the limitations of space, in the style of this exam. The exam is equivalent to the Council of Europe Level B2, and, in the Reading and Writing sections, a candidate would be expected to:

- understand correspondence expressed in non-standard language.
- understand, within a reasonably short period of time, most reports he/she is likely to come across.
- understand the intention of instructions, etc. outside of a factual nature and begin to evaluate, advise, etc.
- make notes that are useful to both him/herself and to colleagues.
- write most letters he/she is likely to be asked to do; such errors as do occur will not prevent understanding of the message.
- write a simple report.

Opposite, you will find a chart showing in detail the skill levels examined in both the Reading and Writing sections of the exam. At the end of this Workbook, on page 76, there is a model letter which has an explanation of the marking scheme. Following the letter, Parts One and Two of the Writing exam are examined, with examples of the type of questions you should expect. Details are also given of the Reading section, with references to units in this book, which will help you further with your exam studies.
There is also a section containing general exam advice on page 79, giving hints and tips to help you improve your technique and your final score.

TEST OF READING

Time: I hour

PART	Main Skill Focus	Input	Response	Number of Questions
1	Reading – scanning and gist	One longer or four shorter informational texts (approx. 250 – 350 words in total)	Matching	7
2	Reading – understanding text structure	Single text: article, report, etc. with sentence level gaps (text plus 7 option sentences approx. 450 – 550 words in total)	Matching	5
3	Reading for gist and specific information	Single text (approx. 450 – 550 words)	4-option multiple choice	6
4	Reading – vocabulary and structure	Single informational text with lexical gaps (text including gapped words approx. 200 – 300 words)	4-option multiple choice cloze	15
5	Reading – understanding sentence structure / error identification	Short text (150 – 200 words) Identification of additional unnecessary words in text	Proof reading	12

TEST OF WRITING

Time: 45 minutes

PART	Functions/Communicative Task	Input	Response	Register
1	E.g., giving instructions, explaining a development, asking for comments, requesting information, agreeing to requests	Rubric only (plus layout of output text type)	Internal communication (medium may be note or message or memo or e-mail) (40 – 50 words)	Neutral/ informal
2	**Correspondence:** e.g., explaining, apologising, reassuring, complaining **Report:** describing, summarising **Proposal:** describing, summarising, recommending, persuading	One or more pieces of input from: business correspondence (medium may be letter, fax or e-mail), internal communication (medium may be note, memo or e-mail), notice, advert, graphs, charts, etc. (plus layout if output is fax or e-mail)	Business correspondence (medium may be letter, fax or e-mail) or short report or proposal (medium may be memo or e-mail) (120 – 140 words)	Neutral/ formal

Career Management

Language Focus 1

Modal Verbs

Modal verbs, such as *can, could, may, might, must, will, would, shall, should, ought, need* and *have* are unusual in English because they do not appear to obey the same rules as other verbs. They generally follow their own set of rules instead, although *need, ought* and *have* can also behave like conventional verbs in some circumstances.

The modal verb *can* is used in the quotation below to express possibility.
'The only thing a man **can** *do for eight hours a day is work.'*
William Faulkner

With the same meaning, Faulkner could also have said,
The only thing it is possible for a man to do eight hours a day is work.

Faulkner also uses the negative form of *can* as follows:
'He **can't** *eat for eight hours.'*

It would mean the same thing to say, *It is not possible for him (a man) to eat for eight hours a day.*

Here are some points to remember about the modal verb *can*.
It does not have an 's' on the third person singular.
He **can**.

The subject and verb are reversed to make a question form.
Can *he?* (Not: *Does he can?*)

It is followed by a infinitive.
I **can go** *to London next week.* (Not: *I can to go*)

It does not have infinitives; other expressions have to be substituted.
I want **to be able to** *keep my job options open.* (Not: *I want to can keep …*)

It is negative when *not* is placed after *can*.
I **cannot** *go to the meeting on Friday.*

It is often replaced with other expressions for future forms.
Next year, I **will be able to** *buy a new house.*
Next year, I **shall** *buy a new house.*

Here are examples of exceptions with *need* and *ought*.

For positive statements, the modals *ought, need* and *have/have got* are followed by an infinitive with *to*. We **ought to advertise** the job. We **need to appoint** a new manager. We **have/have got to appoint** a new manager.

Ⓐ **Use** *can, could* **and** *shall/will be able,* **as well as their negative and question forms to complete the following sentences.**

1. . . . . you hire some temporary staff?
   I . . . . last week, but I . . . . now.

2. We . . . . go to the conference after all.

3. . . . . we issue a short-term employment contract to solve the problem?

4. If I pass my MBA, I . . . . to improve my career prospects.

5. We . . . . hire the cleaners on a temporary basis, ... we?

6. . . . . the new secretary type? Yes, but he . . . . do shorthand.

7. . . . . (you) to work with him as a boss?
   He . . . . be insufferable.

8. I . . . . speak French when I was at school, but I . . . . now. I've forgotten it.

9. . . . . (we) to balance the job losses with job-creation elsewhere?

10. . . . . any of us escape the rat race – I don't think we . . . . !

Language Focus 2

Could

Here are some points to remember about the modal verb *could*.

Could is used when talking about a past ability, in reference to extended periods of time or habitual activities.
She could swim when she was six.

Could is not used when talking about a past possibility, in reference to a single moment or experience. Other expressions, such as *was able to*, have to be substituted. This is always the case when the phrase *managed to [do something]* can be used.
*The driver avoided the accident because he **was able to** stop in time.*
*The driver avoided the accident because he **managed to** stop in time. (**Not**: ... could stop ...)*

Could is used **negatively**, to express something that was **not** possible in a past moment or experience.
*The accident happened because the bus **couldn't** stop.*

This may also be expressed as,
*The accident happened because the bus **was unable to** stop.*

Could as the past of *can* has a separate meaning from *could* when used for polite requests and in a conditional sense.
***Could** you help me with this?*

A Use *was/were able to* or *could* to complete the following.

1. He . . . . get the job because he was well-qualified.
2. He . . . . play the piano when he was six.
3. She succeeded because she . . . . make powerful friends on the way.
4. They . . . . fire him because he never obeyed the dress code.
5. He . . . . hire and fire staff when he worked for Sheppertons.
6. The company . . . . attract the high fliers because it paid huge bonuses.
7. They . . . . cancel the contract because of the penalty clause.
8. She . . . . play tennis extremely well at university.
9. The new employee . . . . fit in very well.
10. The agents got the order and . . . . turn the tables on their competitors.

B Use *couldn't* or *was/were unable to* to complete the following.

1. The company lost the contract as it . . . . re-engineer the project.
2. Unfortunately, he . . . . use his expertise in the new office environment.
3. The co-founder of the company . . . . attend the meeting.
4. We just . . . . reach agreement on anything.
5. Regrettably, the interviewee . . . . keep the appointment.

C Use *could* or *couldn't* to complete the following.

1. If I present the management seminar, ... you handle the discussion afterwards?
2. The interview was tough and the candidate . . . . answer the questions.
3. A government department . . . . do it, but an entrepreneur . . . .
4. If the contract arrives, ... you please forward it to me?
5. Many older staff . . . . adjust to the modern need for job sharing.
6. He . . . . accept that he would never reach the top of the corporate ladder.
7. If I advertise the job, ... you arrange the interviews?
8. The skills shortage . . . . eventually cause us to close the factory.
9. . . . . I speak to the buyer, please? Sorry, he's in a meeting, ... you call back?
10. . . . . you retire early? No, I . . . . because the stock market crashed.

Language Development

The Seven Point Plan was originally devised by the occupational psychologist Professor Alec Rodger to help with career guidance. Rodger's Seven Point Plan has come to be widely used by employers in their business of recruitment and selection. To find the right person for a job, employers first analyse the job, and based on that analysis define the person they are looking for. Employers ask themselves:

What are the results a job-holder is paid to achieve?
What activities does the job-holder engage in to achieve those results?
What does the job demand in terms of the points in Rodger's plan?

The Seven Point Plan is also extremely useful for potential employees. Use of the plan enables a job applicant to carry out a detailed self-analysis before attending an interview. Try the test yourself by asking:
What am I like? (Not: What would I like to be like?)
What are my strengths and weaknesses?
How does my personal employment history fit the requirements of the job?
Am I making the right career choice?

1. Physical make-up:
   general health, strength, appearance, manner, speaking voice, eyesight, height, dexterity and mobility.

2. Attainments:
   qualifications, education and training and/or experience.

3. General intelligence - Innate ability:
   the ability to cope with life's problems, effective functioning of the mind, logical thinking, creative thinking, thinking with words, symbols and codes or things.

4. Special aptitudes:
   linguistic, artistic, spatial ability, verbal, manual and mechanical.

5. Interests:
   hobbies and spare-time activities: social, theoretical and practical.

6. Disposition:
   reliability, acceptability, determination, tact and honesty.

7. Circumstances:
   interactions between the job and the jobholder's domestic circumstances, eg hours of work and location.

A Imagine you are a hotel manager and you need a new receptionist. Look at the characteristics below. Circle those that would be important to consider for this job. Then, beside each characteristic, write the point number it matches in Rodger's Seven Point Plan.

6 a friendly manner	___ a nice speaking voice	___ logical thinking
___ smart appearance	___ managerial experience	___ skill with numbers
___ tact and honesty	___ local knowledge	___ marital status
___ a foreign language	___ sports team involvement	___ reliability

Writing

A **Write your Curriculum Vitae (CV) according to the formula set out below. Try to keep all the information on one A4 page.**

(It is usual to include two referees – two professional people who know you and who can give you a character reference.)

- Your name, home address, phone number and e-mail address.
- Your age and marital status (married – single – divorced) and whether you have children. (No photo unless specifically requested.)
- Job history, starting with your current employment, and your previous employers with dates, leaving no unexplained gaps. If this is your first application for a job, give details of your schools and university or college.
- qualifications, academic and professional
- specialist knowledge
- hobbies and interests
- referees

B **Assuming you are successful with your application, and you are called for interview, your prospective employer may ask you to describe your own personality. Identify the meanings of the adjectives in the box, and then match them to the definitions below. The first has been done for you.**

thoughtful	kind	sensible	lively	calm
honest	cheerful	sociable	optimistic	sympathetic
generous	warm	outgoing	patient	reliable
efficient	hard-working	confident	independent	responsible

1.	thinks of others and is kind and helpful	*thoughtful*
2.	a truthful person	....
3.	ready to share things with others	....
4.	doesn't feel shy in social situations	....
5.	will listen to problems and tries to relate to your difficulties	....
6.	never loses his or her temper, even when faced with stupidity	....
7.	never aggressive	....
8.	usually happy, never miserable	....
9.	always active and full of life	....
10.	does not need advice or help	....
11.	never does anything silly	....
12.	doesn't get nervous or irritated in a difficult situation	....
13.	thinks the future will be wonderful	....
14.	usually busy and does lots of work	....
15.	friendly and enjoys the company of people	....
16.	always arrives for appointments on time	....
17.	can be trusted to take the right decisions	....
18.	caring, gentle and helpful to others	....
19.	shows affection or love for other people	....
20.	always does work well without mistakes	....

UNIT 2 Enterprise

Language Focus 1

Articles

Here are some points to remember about using articles.

The indefinite article (*a* or *an*) is used:
- before singular, countable, non-specific nouns; to refer to one of many.
  an IT consultant, a company employee, a good price

- with some measurements.
  a cup of milk, a dozen eggs

- before some numerical categories.
  a dozen, a hundred, a thousand, a million

The definite article (*the*) is used:
- for a specific noun; where there is only one.
  the sun, the moon, the East (as a region), the only father I ever had, the boss

- for a noun that is specific in context, for example, after a person or thing has been identified in conversation.
  A man spotted a gap in the market. The man is now a wealthy entrepreneur.

The zero article (no article) is used:
- before plural nouns, to convey a general sense.
  Entrepreneurs (in general) come in all shapes and sizes.

- before non-countable nouns, such as materials or commodities, used in a general sense.
  Timber is exported from Malaysia, and iron ore is mined in Australia.

- before abstract nouns that convey a general sense.
  Nature is all around us.
  Space is the final frontier.

A Insert *a/an* or use the zero article as necessary.

1. Jeff Bezos is . . . . entrepreneur who started . . . . on-line bookstore.

2. . . . . risk-taker is . . . . dangerous person to know.

3. . . . . Internet travel agent is the best place to find . . . . information.

4. He invented . . . . ingenious device for the mobile phone.

5. The manager asked for . . . . advice on . . . . whole range of subjects.

6. He works for . . . . computer company; he is . . . . engineer.

7. Does she have . . . . time to read all her e-mails?

8. He is . . . . dotcom millionaire and he gives donations to charity.

9. Can I pay by cheque or must I use . . . . credit card?

10. Do you have to be . . . . lucky person to make . . . . fortune on the stock market?

Language Focus 2

Here are some points to remember about using articles with names.

The definite article (*the*) is used:

- before the name of a country made up of smaller states.
  the United Kingdom, **the** United States, **the** Netherlands

- before a group of islands.
  the Philippines, **the** Galapagos, **the** West Indies

- before rivers, oceans, mountain chains and compass points.
  the Rhine, **the** Seine, **the** Pacific, **the** Pyrenees, **the** Alps
  the north

- before an institution whose name is part of a category.
  the University of California (category: universities of California), **the** Academy of Fine Arts (category: fine arts)

- before famous hotels.
  the Ritz, **the** Hilton, **the** Sheraton

The zero article is used:

- for names of people, countries and institutions or businesses.
  Juliet, Japan, Oxford University, Luigi's Italian Restaurant

- For names that include **lake**, **cape** and **mount**.
  Lake Leman, Mount Kenya, Cape Horn

A Insert *the* or use the zero article as necessary.

1. . . . . youngest manager went to . . . . London School of Economics.

2. . . . . study of . . . . production and use of . . . . wealth is called . . . . Economics.

3. Could you order a new computer? . . . . 746 is a good model, I believe.

4. Whiz-kids sometimes make . . . . wrong decisions and lose money.

5. . . . . Managing Director is staying at . . . . Southbank Hotel tonight.

6. Is that near . . . . Lake Larkin?

7. We invested in an ecotourism company on . . . . Amazon River.

8. Are you going to . . . . Seychelles first or to . . . . India?

9. Is this . . . . one you mean or is it . . . . other one?

10. . . . . sales rep you met at the convention works in . . . . east of . . . . country.

B Insert *the, a, an* or use the zero article as necessary.

(1) . . . . famous ship sailed across (2) . . . . Lake Turana and collected a cargo of (3) . . . . copper ore. It returned to (4) . . . . Pacific Ocean via (5) . . . . Atara Canal. (6) . . . . captain enjoyed this route because he loved (7) . . . . nature, especially (8) . . . . rich flora and fauna on (9) . . . . banks of (10) . . . . canal itself. He loved to watch (11) . . . . moon in (12) . . . . sky above his ship, and often marvelled at (13) . . . . immensity of (14) . . . . space when seen from (15) . . . . deck of (16) . . . . ship at night.

Language Development

Direct / reported speech

When direct speech is changed to reported speech, the tense will often change. Also, when the speech occurs in a different time or place than when or where it is reported, expressions of time and place can also change. For example, *here* changes to *there*. *This* changes to *that*. *Today* changes to *yesterday*. *Now* changes to *then*.

Compare these sentences.

Direct
John is in a store, talking to Tony.
John: 'I **don't** like the prices **here**.'

Reported
Tony is in the store, telling Eva what John said.
John said he **didn't** like the prices **here**.

Tony is at work, telling Sean what John said at the store.
John said he **didn't** like the prices **there**.

Direct
Elena is talking to Tracy on Friday.
Elena: 'I asked Glenn yesterday.'

Reported
It is Friday, and Tracy is telling Joe what Elena said.
Elena said she asked Glenn **yesterday**.

It is Saturday, and Tracy is telling Susan what Elena said
Elena said she asked Glenn the **day before yesterday**.

A **Read this report of a conversation and write what John and Peter actually said. The first sentence has been started for you.**

John told Peter that he was going to visit the warehouse that afternoon with the sales rep to see some damaged products. Peter said he would go too, but he was going to start a meeting right then. John said he thought they would have to negotiate a refund of the contract price, because the damage was very bad. Peter said he would like John to give him a report as soon as possible, but he would be in his meeting until very late. John told him not to worry, because he would fill him in on the visit the following day.

John:  Peter, I am going to visit the warehouse...
....
....
....
....

Peter: ....
....
....
....

John: ....
....
....
....

Peter: ....
....
....
....

John: ....
....
....
....

Writing

You are a young trainee at a technology college. Your hobby is building electronic circuits and you have put together a revolutionary new product. You have received the following letter advising you to write to Megacorp Ltd, and attempt to interest them in your idea.

A **Write the letter, using 120 - 140 words, paying particular attention to include all the points mentioned. Do not include addresses.**

The Business Advisory Group
Leverton
SZ9 3MM

3 March 2005

Dear Mr Smith

Thank you for your enquiry. Although we are unable to market your product for you directly, we suggest you write to the leading mobile phone manufacturer, Megacorp Ltd, to interest them in your project as your idea is obviously a winner. The following points should be mentioned in your letter:
- You won the Electrical Engineering prize at your college for best new ideas in electronic control circuitry when you were 15 years old.
- You are looking for financial backing for a new design which will revolutionise the mobile phone industry.
- You need to take the initiative as soon as possible because you have seen a gap in the market.
- You have taken professional advice and the product is viable.
- Your business plan is enclosed with your letter.

We are sure you will succeed as a young entrepreneur due to your drive, determination and faith in your product. We wish you every success for the future. Our fee, as agreed, will be invoiced directly to you within the next two weeks.

Yours sincerely

A. N. Advisor
New Projects Manager

B You have received the following minutes of a meeting which record a conversation between your Managing Director (MD) and the Publicity Director (PD).

Write an e-mail, using roughly 60 words, to the members of your department, using reported speech to explain the action which is to be taken. Remember to keep the language informal as you are writing an e-mail to your colleagues.

MD: The new model is now ready.

PD: That's good news. We can start the advertising campaign next week.

MD: Let's see, today is Wednesday. I'll finalise the details tomorrow.

PD: Have they changed the specification which you gave me last week?

MD: No, it's the same one I gave you three weeks ago.

PD: OK, I may be able to get some hard-copy to you by next week.

MD: Now, let's move on to the problems in the car park!

To: Department Group
Subject: Meeting Minutes

The MD said that the new model was ready

E-business

Language Focus 1

Question Forms

The word order of questions is often confused, and care should be taken to avoid common mistakes, such as 'What means the word Nethead?' The correct way to ask this question is, 'What **does** the word Nethead **mean**?'

Here are some points to remember about question forms.

• If there is an auxiliary verb, such as *be*, or a modal auxiliary verb, such as *can* or *will*, or in the perfect tenses, question forms can be made simply by reversing the subject and verb order.
You are a computer programmer, becomes, ***Are you** a computer programmer?*
You can programme computers, becomes, ***Can you** programme computers?*
You have programmed computers, becomes, ***Have you** programmed computers?*

• If an auxiliary verb is not present, the question is constructed using *do, does,* or *did.*
You know how to program computers, becomes ***Do you** know how to program computers?*

• Tag questions are made by making a statement, and then tagging on the subject and verb in reversed order.
You are a computer programmer, ***aren't you**?*

• Many questions begin with a question word, such as *why, when, how, what, whose, which,* and *where.*
***Where** did you study computer programming?*

A Turn these statements into questions.

1. I deal in all kinds of IT and Hi-Tech shares.
   ....
2. Martha Lane-Fox is a dotcom millionaire.
   ....
3. He lost money in the great dotcom crash.
   ....
4. I do a lot of e-business these days.
   ....
5. The company de-bugs mainframe computers.
   ....
6. She registered the Web site with the major search engines.
   ....

B Re-order the following statements, and then reverse the subject and verb to make a tag question. The first has been done for you.

1. Net the you are on frequently   *You are frequently on the Net, aren't you?*
2. computer a genius you are   ....
3. computer you literate are   ....
4. over phenomenon is dotcom the   ....
5. banks never Anna online   ....
6. can't life Internet the replace   ....

C Use question words to supply questions to the following answers.

1. ....
   The abbreviation stands for Information Technology.
2. ....
   I think it's about 50 kilometres to London.
3. ....
   Fifty kilos, including the monitor and printer.
4. ....
   The market began to go pear-shaped in 1990.
5. ....
   He said the system is secure for digital payments.
6. ....
   I think Peter's wife is called Mary.
7. ....
   Because its business strategy is poor.
8. ....
   I worked in the IT department for three years.
9. ....
   I found it on Yahoo, after a long search on the web.
10. ....
   I like their home page because it's so well laid out.

Language Focus 2

In the modern office environment we all have to rely on our computers to communicate through the Internet. But how well do we know our machines?

A Choose one of the options below each definition to fill the gap.

1. The gadget for interfacing with our computer is called a . . . . . .
   a. rat   **b.** mouse   **c.** vole

2. A . . . . . . is used under this gadget to provide a flat operating surface.
   a. mat   **b.** platen   **c.** carpet

3. A . . . . . . is the area on screen in which work is typed.
   a. manuscript **b.** document   **c.** deed

4. Documents are kept in a . . . . . .
   a. dossier   **b.** roll   **c.** folder

5. Folders are stored in a . . . . . .
   a. catalogue   **b.** directory   **c.** list

6. Commands are stored on a drop-down . . . . . .
   a. fare   **b.** strip   **c.** menu

7. To remove unwanted text, you press the . . . . . . key.
   a. delete   **b.** erase   **c.** remove

8. To make a copy of an item, you select . . . . . on the drop-down menu.
   a. double   **b.** copy   **c.** duplex

9. Standard business letters in the UK are written on . . . . . . paper.
   a. B5 letter   **b.** US legal   **c.** A4 letter

10. The gap in the text at the beginning of a paragraph is a/an . . . . . .
    a. indent   **b.** recess   **c.** dent

11. Small letters used in text are classified as . . . . . .
    a. suit case   **b.** lower case **c.** brief case

12. Capital letters are classified as . . . . . .
    a. upper class **b.** upper case
    c. middle class

13. To produce heavy type, select the command . . . . . . from the drop-down menu.
    a. brave   **b.** bold   **c.** plucky

14. To place a line under text select . . . . . .
    a. understudy **b.** underscore **c.** underline

15. . . . . . . means the name of the print style you wish to use.
    a. Type   **b.** Pattern   **c.** Font

16. When you want text to align left or right, you use the command . . . . . .
    a. defend   **b.** justify   **c.** prove

17. . . . . . . is a printers' term referring to the size of the print characters.
    a. Sharp   **b.** Direct   **c.** Point

18. The colour . . . . . . is used to apply colour to text and pictures.
    a. palette   **b.** plate   **c.** highlight

19. To play action games where fine control is needed, a . . . . . . is used.
    a. joystick   **b.** slapstick   **c.** lipstick

20. To remove an item the command . . . . . . may be used.
    a. slash   **b.** slice   **c.** cut

Language Development

A Read the text about the dotcom shares, and use the sentences below to fill in each of the gaps. Do not use any sentence more than once.

The Great Dotcom Scam

(1) _The stock market crash_ . . . of the early 21st century may have been a disaster for some investors who thought they had found a money tree which would produce riches and returns for ever. Dealers in the City said you only had to find a new dotcom company, buy the shares, sit back and wait for the profits to flood in – even a fool could see that. **(2)** . . . . of the big banks were advising – the same banks, incidentally, who were responsible for floating the dotcom shares on the world stock exchanges in the first place.

(3) . . . . to unreservedly recommend Internet shares fed a feeding frenzy not seen since the 1929 New York Wall Street crash. **(4)** . . . . and flooded the bull markets with 'buy' orders. Strangely, there was an uncanny parallel with the 1929 crash, which was also conveniently forgotten in the rush to get into Internet businesses. Radio underwent great development during the 1920s and was hailed as the new revolutionary technology. **(5)** . . . . of the day, and, like the Internet, was going to revolutionise the business world.

(6) . . . . boom and bust goes back further than 1929.
(7) . . . . the markets of what was to come. In 1721 the South Sea Company – a company set up to import silver and exotic goods from South America – failed in the same spectacular way. **(8)** . . . . dragged in the investors, but nobody ever made money out of virtual profits. Even before the South Sea bubble burst, Dutch investors had been ripped off in the 17th century by the surge in demand for tulip bulbs. The phenomenon of 'Tulipamania' showed what could happen when perceived profits appeared to create mountains of money. Given that this kind of investment was new in the 17th century, the Dutch investors may have had some excuse for what happened. **(9)** . . . . in the greed-driven society of the late 1990s with the inevitable bust following boom.
(10) . . . . does differ from earlier crashes because it has left in its wake a revolution in business communications. **(11)** . . . . e-mail and a mobile phone for business transactions and to chat with their friends? IT allows us to check out a book price online at Amazon.com before we pay too much for it at the check-out of our local bookstore. **(12)** . . . . to be answered before the great e-commerce revolution is complete, if web pages are to become no more than just electronic catalogues.

a. The stock market crash	**g.** But the lesson was ignored
b. But investors ignored history	**h.** Who now does not use
c. The phenomenon of the stock market	**i.** The legacy of the great dotcom crash
d. The potential for profit	**j.** That is what the financial analysts
e. Two other events should have warned	**k.** The radio set was the new magic
f. The tendency of the analysts	**l.** But there are still many questions

Writing

Your boss is going to travel to Nantes, France to meet a client, and will then stay for one week in the area. He will need to hire a car while he is there. His favourite car is a Mercedes, but your company is having a strict economy drive and a limit has been placed on car hire at 300 Euros per week for all executives. He has asked you to study the following web sites to see which company offers the best car hire deal.

Rentabanger.co.uk   Cars rented worldwide from Minis to Limos. Our cars are nearly new and all come with breakdown cover and an instruction manual in case you experience any small problems. Why not hire one of our vintage oil-eaters if you really are on a budget? Prices start at 100 Euros per week. E-mail Mike the mechanic for further info (at lunch 1-2 p.m.).

BagnolesRus.co.fr   Vehicles available at all major French airports. We specialise in supplying good, reliable second-hand cars. Special offer at Nantes airport on E class Mercedes 400 Euros, but hurry, offer closes at the end of this week.

Reliablerunners.co.fr   Guaranteed new cars always available. We operate from all major French railway stations and offer exceptional value for money. Taxi costs from airports refunded against your hire fee. Discounts for company executives (business card required) and prices start as low as 280 Euros for a four-door car with climatisation.

Burnemup.co.fr   This is the organisation for the executive who needs image and attitude. Impress your clients with a car from our range of super sports models. Want a flashy Boxter, Lexus or Merc? – no problem. Prices from 500 Euros a week, with 1,000 Euro deposit required. E-mail soon – have a nice day.

A **Write a report, in 120-140 words, recommending your choice of car hire company. Explain why your recommendation is the best choice. Remember that headings are not counted in the word total for exam purposes. Set the report out as follows:**

Title
Proceedings
Findings
Recommendations
your signature and job title (be imaginative!)
date

Brand Management

Language Focus

The Present simple, Present continuous and Past simple tenses

In the first paragraph of the article discussing Brand Wars, the Present simple, Present continuous, and Past simple tenses are mixed together in a way which may seem illogical on first reading.

Here are some points to remember about these three tenses.

The Present simple:
- is used for universal truths.
  *Water **boils** at 100 degrees Centigrade.*

- is used for habitual actions.
  *We **sell** $1m worth of our product every week.*

- usually has an 's' on the end of the third person verb.
  *She **sells** only top brands.*

- does not have an 's' in the third person when there is a modal verb.
  *That advertising company **can make** your brand famous.*

The Present continuous:
- is formed with the Present simple of the verb *to be* plus a present participle.
  *Extra millions **are pouring** into R&D.*

- is used for action beginning in the past, continuing into the future, and which is still continuing at the moment of speaking.
  *Counterfeit products **are costing** us a lot of money.*

- is used to express the future.
  *We **are going** to saturate the market with our own brand.*

- is not usually used with verbs such as:
  see, hear, feel, taste, own and *need*

The Past simple:
- is used for an action completed in the past.
  *Phillip Morris **knocked** 40c **off** a packet of Marlboro.*

- is used for habitual actions in the past.
  *We **made** a fortune in our little corner shop because we **opened** all day, every day of the week.*

A Put the verbs in brackets into the Present simple tense.

1. A lot of fake products (come) .... into our markets.
2. We always (prosecute) .... the manufacturers if we can find them.
3. Luxury branded goods (be) .... at the top of the hit list.
4. If Ms Smith (want) .... top quality, she usually (come) .... to us.
5. Our South London sales rep (have) .... good sales figures every month.
6. The market value this week (be) .... $100m.
7. The supermarket always (sell) .... bread as a loss leader.
8. Where do you live? I (live) .... in Zurich.
9. Busy Burgers generally (hold) .... the biggest market share.
10. Market saturation (remain) .... the biggest single threat.

B Put the verbs in brackets into the Present continuous tense.

1. Brand stretching policies (generate) .... higher brand awareness.
2. The Corporate Affairs Department (handle) .... the matter.
3. The MD (live) .... in Denham Village at the moment.
4. We (make) .... good profits this year.
5. Sales (soar) .... this month and we (go) .... to hit our target.
6. We (take) .... a time out for six months.
7. Why (pour / they still) .... money into advertising?
8. Subliminal advertising (increase) .... all the time.
9. Big brands (not give in) .... without a fight.
10. Today, consumer protection (make) .... a difference.

C **Put the verbs in brackets into the Past simple tense.**

1. The consumer durables sector (achieve) . . . . record sales last year.

2. Retail chains (take over) . . . . most of the Moma and Papa stores.

3. The communist government (introduce) . . . . a free market economy.

4. The company (have) . . . . serious problems with the patent rights.

5. In the '90s, the currency dealers always (play) . . . . for high stakes.

6. Last year, the economy (go) . . . . into free fall.

7. Shares (dive) . . . . on the stock market yesterday.

8. The CEO (shoot down) . . . . the marketing department's proposal.

9. A few orders (trickle in) . . . . , but not enough to allow us to avoid bankruptcy.

10. A ballpark figure (be) . . . . all that they (quote) . . . .

D **Put the verbs in brackets into the Present simple or Present continuous tense.**

Proposal to take over JPP Biscuits

The Aim : JPP **(1)** . . . . (be) the brand leaders and they **(2)** . . . . (have) about 40% of the chocolate biscuit market in the UK. We **(3)** . . . . (make) every effort to counter competition from them, but every year they **(4)** . . . . (grow) stronger and they **(5)** . . . . (eat) into our confectionery market. The Chairman **(6)** . . . . (investigate) the possibility of raising shareholder capital and if he **(7)** . . . . , (succeed) he **(8)** . . . . (go) to try to persuade the Board to make a hostile takeover bid. The company **(9)** . . . . (need) to defend market share, and a bid **(10)** . . . . (seem) to be a sensible solution.

Benefits : JPP **(11)** . . . . (build) a new depot which **(12)** . . . . (be) very close to our distribution centre in Northampton. The Transport Department **(13)** . . . . (think) of buying a new fleet of lorries because it **(14)** . . . . (suffer) from the disadvantage of ageing vehicles which **(15)** . . . . (need) a high maintenance budget. Taking over the new facility **(16)** . . . . (make) perfect sense because it **(17)** . . . . (go) to give us excellent access to their distribution network.

Action : Assuming the Board does not **(18)** . . . . (shoot down) the Chairman's proposals, the Finance Department **(19)** . . . . (go) to make arrangements with our bankers to get the flow of capital moving. This will allow a quick raid on JPP shares before they **(20)** . . . . (realise) what **(21)** . . . . (happen)

Language Development

(A) **Fill the gaps with the words given below.**

Familiar icons

It is very easy to think of a number of products which are familiar to us as **(1)** . . . . brands which we recognise, no matter where we are in the world. **(2)** . . . . advertising, product placement (as in the latest James Bond film) and energetic marketing campaigns **(3)** . . . . that the names of Levi, Ray Ban, Harley Davidson, Lotus, Sony and Coke are now familiar **(4)** . . . . names.

But there is one **(5)** . . . . which is well on the way to classic marketing status which achieved its **(6)** . . . . market position in an unconventional way – Häagen-Dazs ice cream. Häagen Dazs was **(7)** . . . . by Ciro in 1961 in New York when sales of their ice cream had slipped back due to increased competition. The company decided to **(8)** . . . . a new product with a finer flavour and texture, smaller pack sizes and an invented, **(9)** . . . . sounding name. The price was deliberately set high to appeal to the **(10)** . . . . end of the market. And instead of spending a **(11)** . . . . on advertising to reach the consumer, news of the desirability of the product was soon spread by **(12)** . . . . through the chattering classes.

Häagen Dazs appeared in up-market locations promoting an image of **(13)** . . . . luxury. Specialist ice cream 'dipping stores' were opened to give people a chance to **(14)** . . . . something which could later be bought in a supermarket. By the early 1980s, Häagen Dazs had become America's leading super-premium ice cream. It was sold to the **(15)** . . . . Pillsbury and later taken over again by the British company Grand Metropolitan. Money was then **(16)** . . . . into advertising to place the product next to other brand **(17)** . . . . . . such as fast cars, jewellery and diamond watches. Semi-erotic **(18)** . . . . were also used to **(19)** . . . . the product's sex appeal. The rest is history. Häagen Dazs has now joined the **(20)** . . . . of the super-brands, and is familiar to us whether we are in Tokyo, Paris or Moscow.

1.	**a.** winning	**b.** chief	**c.** leading
2.	**a.** Combative	**b.** Aggressive	**c.** Bellicose
3.	**a.** practice	**b.** assure	**c.** ensure
4.	**a.** houseboat	**b.** housemaid	**c.** household
5.	**a.** brand	**b.** make	**c.** line
6.	**a.** conspicuous	**b.** prominent	**c.** noticeable
7.	**a.** evolved	**b.** developed	**c.** expanded
8.	**a.** launch	**b.** lunch	**c.** float
9.	**a.** erotic	**b.** esoteric	**c.** exotic
10.	**a.** opulent	**b.** extravagant	**c.** luxury
11.	**a.** ransom	**b.** fortune	**c.** mint
12.	**a.** foot and mouth	**b.** mouth	**c.** word of mouth
13.	**a.** ashamed	**b.** unashamed	**c.** shameless
14.	**a.** sample	**b.** test	**c.** try on
15.	**a.** multi-cultural	**b.** multi-talented	**c.** multi-national
16.	**a.** pumped	**b.** pushed out	**c.** emptied
17.	**a.** idols	**b.** figures	**c.** icons
18.	**a.** pictures	**b.** snaps	**c.** images
19.	**a.** promote	**b.** encourage	**c.** hold up
20.	**a.** files	**b.** strata	**c.** ranks

Writing

A Look carefully at the sales letter below. Circle and correct the mistakes in style, punctuation and spelling.

Logan Garages
London Road
Logan Town
ZZ7 7ZZ

The Managing Director,
Electronic Circuits Ltd,
Legend Street,
Logan Town.

Twenty first march 2005

dear sir or madam

Wud you lik to be the oner of a supper new 4X4 family roadster
Be the envy of your frends and order the modle with the metalic
paint.

But hurry; this ofer is limited to the first twenti ordres recieved
befor midnite on friday. Send the repli paid cuopon in the envalope
provided to us at Grotty Garages without delay to benifit from our
unrepeatible offer.

Rememember this car is going to be the won everyone wants so
don't mis out.
Truly yours
sells manger
V. Grimy-Hands
s.p. why not aks for a test drove at your conveneince

Language Focus 1

Logical Connectors

Read this sentence which begins with a logical connector: **Since** *the only legitimate object of doing business is to make a decent profit, few things can be as important as the price tag you put on what you sell.*

In this sentence, the word *since* introduces a well-known reason that explains important information in the second part of the sentence.

Here are some points to remember about the logical connectors *since, as,* and *because.*

Since

- It presents a well-known reason in the **first** part of the sentence.
- It explains and stresses the information in the **second** part of the sentence.
- A comma separates the first and second parts of a sentence that uses *since.*
  Since the company has had a profitable year, we will all receive substantial bonuses.

As

As could have been used instead of *since,* although it is slightly less formal:
As *the company has had a profitable year, we will all receive substantial bonuses.*

Because

- It generally presents a reason in the **second** part of the sentence.
- It explains and stresses the information in the **first** part of the sentence.
  *The profits doubled **because** the marketing strategy was brilliant.*
- It **only** follows a comma

when it explains a **belief**.
*We will probably have to drop the price, **because** I can't see any other way to gain market share.*

Exceptions

In order to emphasise an explanation, newspaper articles sometimes use *because* to present a reason in the first part of a sentence.
This keeps the story flowing and is acceptable journalistic style.
Because *the crime was so terrible, he was sentenced to life in prison.*

A Choose either *since, because* or *as* to complete the following sentences.

1. . . . . the customers were French, a Cordon Bleu meal was prepared.

2. The price is very competitive . . . . we have a special offer this month.

3. . . . . nuclear power is cleaner than coal, we are building more nuclear reactors.

4. We must raise prices . . . . our production costs have escalated.

5. . . . . the figures were wrong, a mistake in the accounts was unavoidable.

6. . . . . we cut our prices last month, it is impossible to give more discount.

7. The retail price index rose . . . . vegetable prices took off.

8. . . . . the government has frozen wages, we cannot give you an increase.

9. . . . . demand fell, a reduction in the workforce was required.

10. . . . . the competition was so fierce, we had to include a free offer with every order.

11. This year is going to be a financial disaster . . . . our product has not yet sold well and it is already October.

B Choose *As* or *Since* to make the sentences formal or informal.

1. . . . . . . we knew them, we allowed a delay in payment of two weeks.

2. . . . . . . money will get you anything, let's make an outrageous bid for the company.

3. . . . . . . he asked me politely, I gave him all the information he required.

4. . . . . . . the figures are absolutely accurate, there can be no mistake.

5. . . . . . . China is becoming a main trading nation, we must open an office in Beijing.

Language Focus 2

Adjectives and adverbs for data and graphs

In the Coursebook on page 49, the words that indicate motion on a graph may be augmented by the use of specific **adjectives** and **adverbs**. These words convey specific information about the action of motion verbs or the quality of motion nouns. As a rule, adjectives describe nouns and adverbs describe either verbs or adjectives.

Here are some points to remember about adjectives and adverbs of motion:
Adverbs of motion generally follow the verb.
*Prices rose **steadily**.*
*The market fell **marginally**.*

Adjectives of motion are generally placed in front of nouns.
*There was a **dramatic** rise in prices.*
*A **marginal** decrease in the market occurred.*

A Use the adjectives and adverbs in the box to complete the stock market report below.

steady	sharply	small	steadily	slight
marginally	strongly	slowly	dramatically	rapidly

Our reporter in the City says there was brisk trading on the FTSE yesterday with a **(1)** ...... rise in the index to 4589. Commodities began **(2)** ...... with a **(3)** ...... increase in the price of oil by three cents a barrel. Surprisingly, bank stocks fell **(4)** ..... which was against the market trend, but the currency traders still expected the dollar to rise **(5)** ...... against the yen. Shares in pharmaceuticals recovered **(6)** ...... after Monday's losses on bid rumours for a major drugs manufacturer. Airlines are suffering with the current uncertainty of the short-haul market, but BA reported a **(7)** ...... increase in profits for the first quarter of the year. The major High Street store groups still continue to benefit from consumer spending and Selbucks **(8)** ...... lifted the sector with its surprise takeover of Smallboys Housewares. Gold fluctuated **(9)** ...... throughout the day, finishing two points up at the close of business. Two late items, just received by our newsdesk: sugar peaked at $400 a tonne, while melon futures soared **(10)** ...... following the devastation of the crop caused by hurricane Petra.

Language Development

(A) **Match the words below to their definitions.**

1. value
    a. made exactly like something else in order to deceive
       bank notes

2. valueless
    b. so high in value that it cannot be calculated
       your mother's love

3. valuable
    c. deceitful behaviour for the purpose of making money
       selling shares in a company which does not exist

4. invaluable
    d. a copy intended to deceive
       a famous painting

5. priceless
    e. the worth of something in money, or in other terms
       a price of £20

6. counterfeit
    f. something which has no value
       shares in a bankrupt company

7. fraud
    g. too valuable for the worth to be measured or impossible to measure with money
       good advice

8. forgery
    h. having a stated value in terms of money
       jewels

9. worth
    i. something which is worth a lot of money
       a gold watch

(B) **Using the words above, fill the gaps in the following text.**

How the value of a commodity can change

Yuri was planning a gap year when he won two prizes of great **(1)** . . . . in a competition. One was a round-the-world air ticket and the other a Rolex watch. Wasting no time, he travelled to Australia. He put on his backpack and hiked out into the desert to look for a goldmine. Unfortunately, he managed to get lost and quickly ran out of food and water. On the sixth day a helicopter appeared and the pilot asked Yuri if he needed water – a **(2)** . . . . commodity in the desert.

Yuri agreed to exchange his Rolex, which had now become **(3)** . . . . to him, for the water. The pilot checked the watch very carefully, in case it was a **(4)** . . . . Yuri assured the pilot he would not commit a **(5)** . . . . in such a desperate situation.
In the helicopter, Yuri tried to exchange his bank notes for the Rolex. But the pilot checked the notes and found they were **(6)** . . . . He told Yuri the watch was **(7)** . . . . more than his offer anyway.

When he arrived back at his hotel, the receptionist offered Yuri some **(8)** . . . . advice. 'Always take plenty of water into the desert,' she told him, 'You never know how **(9)** . . . . it could be!'

Writing

International Shipping terms: Incoterms

When goods and commodities are traded around the world, buyers have to know the prices not only in terms of currency, eg a price in dollars, but the price including all shipping costs so that a net price may be calculated before the addition of a profit margin. The main abbreviations for these terms are shown below.

FOB – Free On Board The price includes all loading charges to get the goods onto a ship, and the price is usually followed by the port of origin, eg. FOB Hamburg.

CANDF – Cost And Freight This includes the basic cost of the goods and the freight (fare) to the destination. The price is usually followed by the destination port, eg. CANDF Rotterdam.

CIF – Cost Insurance and Freight The same as CANDF but with the addition of an insurance premium, to cover any losses in case the ship should sink. The premium is paid by the buyer. This is also followed by the name of a port, eg CIF New York.

FOR – Free On Rail The price of goods after loading onto railway wagons.

FOL – Free On Lorry The price of goods after loading onto a lorry.

FRANCO – Goods delivered freight paid to final destination.

For internal trade within a country the terms used are as follows:

COD – Cash On Delivery

CWO – Cash With Order

PRO-FORMA INVOICE Pre-payment before the goods are despatched.

A Use incoterms to complete the e-mail below:

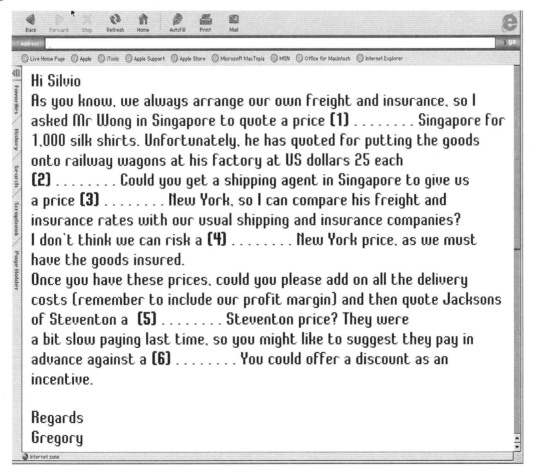

Hi Silvio
As you know, we always arrange our own freight and insurance, so I asked Mr Wong in Singapore to quote a price (1) . . . . Singapore for 1,000 silk shirts. Unfortunately, he has quoted for putting the goods onto railway wagons at his factory at US dollars 25 each (2) . . . . Could you get a shipping agent in Singapore to give us a price (3) . . . . New York, so I can compare his freight and insurance rates with our usual shipping and insurance companies?
I don't think we can risk a (4) . . . . New York price, as we must have the goods insured.
Once you have these prices, could you please add on all the delivery costs (remember to include our profit margin) and then quote Jacksons of Steventon a (5) . . . . Steventon price? They were a bit slow paying last time, so you might like to suggest they pay in advance against a (6) . . . . You could offer a discount as an incentive.

Regards
Gregory

Language Focus

The Imperative Form

English verbs use four basic moods, one of which is the imperative. The imperative is a mood of command or order. It is very useful for business people because it can be used when entertaining, for example, in a restaurant, to politely offer food or drink.

Here are some points to remember about the imperative.

- It has the same form in both the second person singular and plural, and is the same as the infinitive without *to*.
  Have some more raki, Mr Turan.
  Have some more wine, Mr and Mrs Carubin.

- It is made negative by placing *don't* in front of the verb.
  *Please **don't** open the window.*

- It is used as an instruction.
  *To get to the restaurant, **go** along the street and **turn** left.*

- It is used to set a condition.
  ***Suppose** we went to the Chinese restaurant. Would that be OK?*

- It is used as an invitation.
  ***Come** in.*
  ***Have** some rice, Mr Tanaka.*

- It is used as an appeal, cry or supplication.
  ***Help, call** the police!*

- It is used as a suggestion.
  ***Try** the Petite Sardine in Market Street if you want a good restaurant.*

Variations of the imperative for suggestions.

To sound more natural or gentle, the imperative suggestion is often preceded by *let* plus an object pronoun *us*, usually abbreviated to ***let's***.
***Let's try** the Petite Sardine.*

Imperative suggestions with *let* can also be followed by other pronouns, such as *me, him, her, us* and *them*.
***Let me** help you with that.*

To make a negative, two forms are used.
***Let's not** worry about the bill.* (more formal)
***Don't let's** worry about the bill.* (less formal)

A Insert the correct imperative from the box below into the gaps.

wash	enjoy	pour	chop
shake	cut (2)	place	sprinkle
slice	add	take	mix
crisp	peel	toss	season

A group of business colleagues went to a restaurant to conclude their negotiations. Once the deal had been finalised, a heated discussion developed about the best way to prepare a salad. They wrote down their conclusions on a napkin as follows:

(1) . . . . all the ingredients very carefully.
(2) . . . . the lettuce in the fridge and then **(3)** . . . . it into thin strips.
(4) . . . . off the excess water and
(5) . . . . it in a bowl. **(6)** . . . .
a carrot and **(7)** . . . . it into thin strips.
(8) . . . . these with the lettuce. **(9)** . . . . .
. . . . an onion very finely and, if you like it,
(10) . . . . a little chopped garlic to the onion. **(11)** . . . . this on top of the other ingredients. **(12)** . . . . in some chopped beetroot, tomatoes and potatoes and
(13) . . . . on a mixture of oil and vinegar to taste. **(14)** . . . . with salt and pepper.
(15) . . . . the salad and **(16)** . . . .

B Choose an imperative form from the box to complete the sentences.

pass	hand	make	close	open	get
order	call	book	ask	have	

1. . . . . the wine and allow it to breathe before we drink it.

2. . . . . the window please, it's cold in the bar tonight.

3. Waiter, ... the bill out to my company, please.

4. . . . . the cream jug along to Claire, please.

5. Could you . . . . me the serving spoon, please?

6. . . . . some of these prawns, they're delicious.

7. . . . . three take-aways, we'll have to eat in the office.

8. John, ... a side salad for Herr Blicken, please.

9. Maria Cristina, ... the waiter for the wine list, please.

10. Edward, ... the restaurant and . . . . a table for five, please.

C Use *let's,* or *let's not* to complete the following suggestions.

1. . . . . go to that new Italian restaurant, it sounds great.

2. The meal's getting cold. . . . . wait.

3. . . . . go to a non-smoking restaurant tonight, for a change.

4. . . . . book a table at the Ritz to really impress our client.

5. . . . . stay too late as we have an important meeting in the morning.

6. . . . . try the special at the Swedish place.

7. Don't rush, ... savour it.

8. . . . . wait until nine o'clock tonight . . . . eat earlier.

9. . . . . offer some hospitality.

10. That meal was phenomenal! . . . . congratulate the chef personally.

D If you really want to impress your English host, you have to know how to make the perfect cup of tea. Select the correct imperatives from the box below to complete these important instructions. Some are used more than once.

take	tip	add	spoon	bring
pour	fill	leave	brew	remember

(1) . . . . a kettle, (2) . . . . it with water and (3) . . . . it to the boil. When the kettle has boiled, (4) . . . . a little hot water into the teapot to warm it.

(5) . . . . the kettle back to the boil. When the pot is warm, (6) . . . . out the water and (7) . . . . one teaspoon of tea for each person. (8) . . . . to add one teaspoon for the pot! (9) . . . . in the hot water and (10) . . . . the teapot to stand. (11) . . . . the tea for about four minutes and then (12) . . . . out the liquid into the cups. (13) . . . . sugar into the cups as required and (14) . . . . milk to taste.

E You have been given the following directions to a restaurant. Underline the imperatives.

Go to the end of Station Road and turn left at the traffic lights. Walk on for 200 metres and then take the first road on your left – cross at the pelican crossing; it's safer. Keep going until you see the Eagle and Child pub. Just past the pub, turn right into the park and follow the path to the main gates. Go through the gate and you will see Luigi's Restaurant directly in front of you. Give the waiter a tip, otherwise he is liable to become unpleasant. Have a nice meal!

Language Development

Idioms

An idiom is an expression which has to be taken as a whole – you cannot translate individual words and make any sense of the phrase. For example, the phrase *it's raining cats and dogs* simply means, *it is raining heavily*. If someone said this, and you looked out of the window, you would be disappointed because you would not see any cats or dogs!

A **There are more idioms in the following text than we would normally use in the course of a conversation, but, as a challenge, try to identify their meanings as you read.**

The Sales Manager was *in a pickle* because he had forgotten to make the reservations. He had to book a table at the most popular restaurant in town otherwise he would *have egg on his face*. His company was trying to *offer a carrot* to a big client to close a deal. Every time he phoned The Grôs Crevette he found the line engaged and he wished *this hot potato* had been given to someone else. As he was *in a jam*, he asked his secretary for help. She told him not to *make a meal out of* booking a meal. Her sister worked at the Grôs Crevette and she could always get *the plum tables*. She said it would be *a piece of cake* to make the arrangements. The Sales Manager thought the whole thing *had gone pear-shaped*, but his secretary had *saved his bacon* once again.

B **Match the following food idioms from the text above with their correct definitions.**

1. to be in a pickle	**a.** something no one wants to handle
2. to have egg on his face	**b.** to be stuck
3. to offer a carrot	**c.** the best ones
4. a hot potato	**d.** to make too big an issue of something
5. to be in a jam	**e.** to tempt someone to move forward
6. to make a meal out of	**f.** to be in a problematic situation
7. the plum tables	**g.** very easy
8. a piece of cake	**h.** to be embarrassed
9. to go pear-shaped	**i.** to resolve someone's problem
10. to save someone's bacon	**j.** to go wrong

Writing

A You have been asked to suggest a different form of corporate entertainment to the usual expensive meal at the local restaurant. First study the advertisements and choose the best four titles from a - g below for each advertisement.

1. We're just 50 miles from London, easy to reach by road and rail. We have 300 acres of flat event space. You can try 4x4s, go-carts, banger races, cross-country motorcycling, army jeeps and balloon flights. You can even bring the kids. Loads of fun guaranteed for stressed executives and their clients.

2. Haze and smoke machine, bubble machine, the very latest pre-releases, high specification sound and light. Pyrotechnics available. Marquees. Rifle shooting. Prom Nights. We are a family-run business with the most up-to-date equipment. We will organise an event for you, or you can hire everything to suit your own arrangements.

3. Visit our Country Barn conversion for that special business event or dinner – a champagne reception perhaps? Built in 1541 by King Henry VIII's master carpenter, our Country Barn offers an ideal, convenient venue to impress your clients. Our first class kitchens and Cordon Bleu chef will provide a bespoke menu to give you a meal to remember.

4. Get the adrenaline pumping behind the wheel of a Humvee or drive a Sherman tank through mud and water in traditional battlefield-simulated conditions. Not tough enough for your clients? Try our mock SAS survival training course. Tailor-made days to suit your company's individual needs. Drive it! Shoot it! Crush it!

a. Traditional rural hospitality	**e.** Conveniently located family fun days
b. Kitchen visits and cooking courses	**f.** Tanks-R-Us
c. Do It Yourself Hi-tech fun and games	**g.** Join the army for a day
d. The ultimate driving experience	

B Complete the sentences, matching the best choices from a to f.

1. Executives and their clients can enjoy…
2. Our equipment brings out the kid in your client because …
3. We know you will enjoy the rural calm of …
4. If you are a good organiser, why not …

a. swimming in an Olympic-style pool.
b. an exciting day out with the family.
c. clay pigeon shooting and Paintball.
d. they will be able to smash things up and lose their inhibitions for a day.
e. our historical setting and peaceful atmosphere.
f. hire our gear, arrange your own event.

C Now write a memo of 30-40 words to your boss, recommending one of the above activities.

Include details of the event, why you think it would be suitable for your company's clients, and a proposed date for the event to take place.

Language Focus 1

The Present perfect tense

This tense is often confused with the Past simple tense, and the rules can be hard to remember. Consequently, English learners frequently make mistakes with the Present perfect tense, such as, *I'm living* in Paris since 1999. The correct way to say this is: *I have lived* in Paris since 1999.

Here are some points to remember about the present perfect tense.

- It is constructed with the auxiliary verb *have* which remains in the present tense, plus **a past participle**.

  *The Design Department **has tackled** the problem.*

- To form a question, the subject and *have* are inverted.

  ***Has** the **Design Department tackled** the problem?*

- To form a negative, **not** is inserted after the auxiliary verb.

  *The Design Department **has not tackled** the problem.*

- It is used for the duration of an action begun in the past and continuing to the present.

  *I **have worked** here for three years.* (I still work here.)

- It is used when we talk about a timeless action.

  *I **have seen** the contract before.* (Compare: *I **saw** the contract last week.*)

- It defines actions which started in the past and which affect the present.

  *He **has invented** a new mousetrap.* (That is why he is receiving an award tonight.)

- In the example above, if we were more concerned with the time the action actually took place, we would use the past tense.

  *Last week, **he invented** a new mousetrap.*

- It is **not** used with terms such as the following, which require the past tense:

  ago, yesterday, last week, then, in 2001

Use with *just, already* and *since*

- It is often accompanied by the word *just,* to emphasise that an activity has been completed in the immediate past.

  *I **have just** discovered a new power source.*

- It is also often accompanied by the word *already*, to emphasise that an act is accomplished.

  *We **have already discussed** that point.* (We don't need to discuss it now.)

- The use of the word *since* almost always requires the present perfect tense.

  *He **has worked** here **since** January.* (Not: *He has worked here since two years*).

A Put the verbs in brackets into the Present perfect tense.

1. The MD (advise) . . . . the Patent Department.

2. Eurotunnel shares (fluctuate) . . . . on the FTSE for two years.

3. The old model (just/fail) . . . . once again.

4. The patent (run out) . . . . after fifty years.

5. Engineering development (be) . . . . a priority with our company.

B Put the verbs in brackets into the question form of the Present perfect tense.

1. How much (the project/cost) . . . . so far?

2. (You/visit) . . . . his workshop and laboratory?

3. (The boss/agree) . . . . to it yet?

4. After spending all that money, (they/kill off) . . . . the scheme?

5. (He/choose) . . . . the best solution?

C Put the verbs in brackets into the negative using the Present perfect.

1. They (sign) . . . . the contract.

2. The buyers (see) . . . . and approved the prototype.

3. The artist (redesign) . . . . the whole advertisement, only the headline.

4. Unfortunately, the major breakthrough (make) . . . . any difference.

5. Your secretary (make) . . . . copies of the plans.

Language Focus 2

Expressing Opinions

Business people are always involved in negotiations and discussions and have a constant need not only to express their own opinions, but also to discover how their colleagues and customers feel about certain issues. Closed questions, that elicit a *yes* or *no* response are best avoided as they are too direct, a little undiplomatic, and do not lead to further discussion. Polite, open-ended question phrases, such as *What do you think about …?* are often much more useful.

Here are several ways to ask for and express opinions. These phrases get more specific or personal as you progress down the lists. The expressions of disagreement also get stronger as you progress down the list.

How to ask for an opinion
What do you think of/about …?
What's your opinion of …?
How do you find …?
How do you feel about …?
Do you agree that …?

How to give an opinion
I think that …
In my opinion …
As I see it …
Speaking personally, I think that …
My view is that …

How to agree strongly
So do I.
I quite agree.
I entirely agree with you.
They certainly should.

How to disagree strongly
I disagree.
I disagree with you entirely.
I'm afraid I don't agree.
I don't agree with you at all.

Yes, …
you're quite right.
that's just how I see it.
that's exactly my opinion.
that's how I feel.
exactly.

No, …
I really can't agree.
I wouldn't accept that.

How to half agree
Well, yes.
Yes, perhaps.
Yes, in a way.
Yes, I agree up to a point.
Yes, I suppose so.
Yes, I dare say you're right.

How to disagree strongly/impolitely
Oh! Come on!
That's rubbish!
You must be joking!
What nonsense!
You can't be serious!
You're not serious, surely?
You can't really mean that!

A Respond to the following statements using one of the above ways to express your opinion.

1. Genetic engineering is a disaster for mankind and experiments should be banned.
   ....

2. English is an easy language to learn.
   ....

3. We need more nuclear power stations.
   ....

4. Now that we have the Internet, we should allow more people to work at home.
   ....

5. Communism is the best system of government because it distributes wealth fairly.
   ....

6. Cosmetic surgery is unnatural and symbolises our obsession with our bodies.
   ....

7. Although computers are a wonderful invention, they have created unemployment.
   ....

8. Capital punishment should be compulsory for murder.
   ....

9. Smoking should not be allowed in bars or restaurants.
   ....

Language Development

A Read the article about innovation and answer the questions below. For each question mark *a* or *b*.

It has often been said that if you could invent a new mousetrap, the world would beat a path to your door. But many companies used to pay little or no attention to investing money in a Research and Development department. They preferred to respond to market forces, waiting until the consumer initiated product development by modifying demand in the market place. This usually resulted in simple fine-tuning of a product's salient features and many missed opportunities.

Manufacturers frequently discovered that innovation had passed them by when it was too late to act. When they finally woke up to the news, they found a competitor had stolen their customers. A frequently heard argument was, '*If it's not broken, don't fix it.*' Unfortunately, it is still a fact that time is seldom devoted in a small business to intense brainstorming sessions to consider the long-term future of a particular product. Manufacturers often find that they've done too little too late.

But companies ignore investment in research at their own peril. The Swiss watch, Swatch, is a prime example of a product which was produced in response to the loss of a market through competition. Japanese manufacturers stole the Swiss watch industry's market, virtually overnight, when they flooded Europe with cheap digital watches. Digital watches were examples of new technology which soon displaced the old–style analogue watches. The Swiss responded with innovation of their own – a fashion watch, produced on automated machines with economies of scale, which reversed the decline of their home industry.

Role models for efficient R&D departments are hard to find, and many managers acknowledge their inability to produce a true blueprint. Finding staff is not easy; people who invent new concepts do not always go to university and gain degrees in innovation. In fact many of the great inventors from history were ordinary people pursuing their own interests. Michael Faraday could never have known how his early experiments in electro-magnetism would influence and shape modern society. Nobody knows how many Faradays work in present day R&D departments. What is clear is that industry has been alerted to the need for continuing research. In the tough business environment of the early 21st century, the command 'Don't just sit there, invent something' has been replaced by hard cash and budgets totalling 20% of turnover to ensure future profitability and company survival.

1. Companies need to innovate because:
   a. new inventions are the life blood of a company and ensure its survival.
   b. consumers are never satisfied with the products they have.
2. Small companies:
   a. use the available time wisely to discuss new concepts and ideas.
   b. do not consider R&D departments as a necessity.
3. Swatch succeeded because:
   a. the Swiss invented the digital watch.
   b. the company developed Japanese technology and interpreted it in a unique way.
4. According to the writer you have to:
   a. have a university degree to be a great inventor.
   b. invest serious money to maintain market share.

Writing

A foreign student was asked to write a memo while working as an assistant. Unfortunately, he was rather confused about the use of the words *do* and *make* and the tenses he should use.

A **Re-write the phrases in his memo that contain errors with *do* and *make*, and verb tense. The first one has been re-written for you.**

As you know, since we are making business with developing countries, it is important to make recommendations to various government departments. Due to intense competition, we are needing to do an impact on our customers and we should must avoid any losses, as profit margins are very small. We have make progress in the past by spend a lot of money on entertaining our clients. If you would need to do a decision on how much to spend, please contact the Finance Department for advice. Comparisons made recently with some of our competitors show that we are not spending enough in this area. The sales force is doing a big effort this month and the MD wants everyone to make some comments, which can to be discussed at the sales meeting. If you want some further information, you only have to do a phone call and I will be pleased to try to make a good job by help you.

Alex

.... since we are doing business ....

....

....

....

....

....

....

....

....

....

....

....

....

B **Read the letter which offers exclusive rights for a new invention. Using your boss's notes in the boxes, write a letter of 120-140 words, politely declining the offer.**

> Upside Down Productions Ltd.
> Railway Arches Back Street
> Birmingham BZ4 2R
>
> 21st September 2005
>
> Dear Sir or Madam
> I am writing to offer you exclusive manufacturing rights of my new mini-underwater TV set, a partnership link-up which will make your company a great deal of money.
>
> We don't manufacture electrical items.
>
> Just think of it. Demand will be huge from deep-sea divers and other people who have to work under water.
>
> I can't see a huge demand at the moment.
>
> No longer will they have to look at the fish for entertainment when they can carry one of our mini-marvels with them. We have already patented this device, but we could allow you to manufacture it under licence.
>
> Exclusive rights only, no licences!
>
> Perhaps we could meet to discuss the royalty fee, say next month.
>
> Diary booked up for foreseeable future.
>
> I do hope you see the huge potential for this product and I look forward to hearing from you.
>
> Yours faithfully
> A. Loony (inventor)

Language Focus 1

Prepositions

Prepositions come before other words, usually nouns or noun phrases.

Here are some points to remember about prepositions.

- They often connect a noun with a verb.
  It was sold for £10.

- Some verbs are often followed by the same preposition, and it is possible to learn the two words as a complete pair.
  agree with somebody
  believe in an idea
  listen to something

A Insert the correct preposition from the box below into the gaps. Some prepositions may be used more than once.

on	in	to	for	by	through	with

1. The company was successful .... changing its image.
2. Oil companies are not respected .... the public because of pollution worries.
3. Our PR Department is superior .... our nearest competitor's.
4. Sales are growing .... wider brand awareness.
5. The post room apologised .... the late delivery of the mail.
6. Fast-food outlets should take responsibility .... disposal of their packaging.
7. We need to change and update .... a new computer system.
8. The Production Department is talking .... the designers at the moment.
9. Our MD is very pleased .... the new advertisements.
10. Good ice cream sales figures are dependent .... fine weather in summer.

B Insert the correct preposition from the box below into the gaps. Some prepositions may be used more than once.

with	on	by	at	of	into	to

1. An informer spoke .... the press and we had some bad publicity.
2. Some Benetton customers were shocked .... the new advertisements.
3. The sales slipped due .... cheaper Far Eastern imports.
4. Don't be afraid .... cyberbuzz. Our spin doctors will deal with it.
5. The test market area was divided .... three zones.
6. Nike responded .... creating a greener image for the company.
7. They decided to share responsibility .... their manufacturing partners.
8. The PR department is very clever .... manipulating the media.
9. New brochures and leaflets always have a positive effect .... sales.
10. A few companies still have difficulties .... global communications.

C Insert the correct preposition from the box below into the gaps. Some prepositions may be used more than once.

to	about	on	by	with	of

1. Our rivals can only dream .... the profits we make.
2. The multi-national company was disappointed .... the court's decision.
3. The lawyers insisted .... going to trial.
4. Now we are faced .... a corporate crisis.
5. Hundreds .... samples were stolen at the trade fair.
6. Our shareholders were all impressed .... the presentation.
7. The newsletter was discontinued due to a lack .... support.
8. Could you explain the analysis .... the Board of Directors on Tuesday?
9. Half .... the money spent on advertising is wasted, but which half?
10. You should listen .... your customers, not the PR department.

Language Focus 2

A Read the text of a mission statement given in an address to an audience of sales representatives by a newly appointed Managing Director. Choose one of the options below to fill the gaps.

'Ladies and Gentlemen of the sales force, we are looking forward to a **(1)** .... future. Our company is well **(2)** .... in the market place and we must maintain our **(3)** .... -class reputation. It is only through the pursuit of **(4)** .... that we can use our ground- **(5)** .... ideas and **(6)** .... -edge technology to keep ahead of our competitors.

Let us project an image of a user- **(7)** .... company which can deliver **(8)** .... quality, combined with **(9)** .... -effective solutions for our clients. We cannot be complacent or allow the competition to even think about stealing our customers. Remember, the new management intends to change and **(10)** .... the company image which has, if I may use a modern **(11)** ...., become a little tired and uncool of late. We did, as you know, suffer some **(12)**......... from the reduction of our range, and mistakes were made. But I intend to **(13)**......... our image and add strength to it to bring **(14)** .... and excitement to our marketing campaigns.

Please read all our **(15)** .... material to familiarise yourselves with our new look and make our **(16)** .... second to none. We can create **(17)** .... value as we advance the frontiers of **(18)** .... In the increasingly borderless world of e-commerce and B2B, where even the remotest of locations is now **(19)** .... connected, we must strive to remain **(20)** .... competitive. We have the products, you have the vision to succeed. Go out there into the market place and bring back the orders!'

1.	a. booming	b. mushrooming	c. fruitful	d. successful
2.	a. understood	b. respected	c. honoured	d. trusted
3.	a. high	b. working	c. world	d. second
4.	a. eminence	b. strength	c. excellence	d. distinction
5.	a. cutting	b. shaping	c. breaking	d. lifting
6.	a. slicing	b. paring	c. cutting	d. chopping
7.	a. matey	b. amicable	c. hospitable	d. friendly
8.	a. high	b. eminent	c. elevated	d. steep
9.	a. price	b. cost	c. charge	d. value
10.	a. out-take	b. date	c. in-put	d. update
11.	a. preposition	b. synonym	c. idiom	d. antonym
12.	a. destruction	b. harm	c. wound	d. damage
13.	a. reinforce	b. hold onto	c. support	d. uphold
14.	a. force	b. power	c. energy	d. life
15.	a. confidential	b. brochure	c. publicity	d. hype
16.	a. name	b. regard	c. reputation	d. standing
17.	a. shareholder	b. stockholder	c. bondholder	d. broker
18.	a. science	b. technology	c. experiment	d. innovation
19.	a. electronically	b. wireless	c. wire	d. mechanically
20.	a. so	b. highly	c. much	d. greatly

Language Development

A Kelly Haddon, who works for the IEE in London, was asked what exactly she did in the day-to-day activities of her job as a Public Relations manager. Here are some of her comments. Read the text and find equivalents for the words in italics from the box below.

workers	description	processes	moral	spread
statements	pamphlets	tactful	concept	offices
occasion	area	governmental	conversation	
certification	occupation	principles	appraises	
association	approval	newspapers and TV		

There is a **(1)** *definition* of Public Relations which says it is the management function which **(2)** *evaluates* public attitudes, identifies the policies and procedures of an individual or **(3)** *organisation* with public interest, and plans and executes a programme of action to earn public understanding and **(4)** *acceptance*. Depending on the area in which a manager works, Public Relations efforts try to establish open **(5)** *dialogue* and create positive relations with other organisations, government, the **(6)** *media*, the public at large and internal bodies of **(7)** *employees*.

We are information managers and we employ many writing **(8)** *methods*. Of course, newspapers and magazines are regularly used, but the Internet now plays an increasing role in the way we **(9)** *disseminate* information. Some of the other tools we use are press releases, backgrounders and press kits, public service **(10)** *announcements*, articles, annual reports, speeches and presentations, editorials, flyers and **(11)** *brochures*, and finally, advertising and branding.

The big money is earnt by the managers who work in investor relations. They deal with shareholders of the really important companies and the work involves a lot of **(12)** *image* management. We also have to deal with the press – media relations – and a lot of companies have **(13)** *departments* which look after internal communications with their own employees. **(14)** *Event* management can form part of our work, and this is not always for profit because sometimes charity organisations are involved. A very large area of Public Relations work is carried out for governments and the public service **(15)** *sector*. And a major area of PR is in international relations where we help people communicate across national borders. A lot of **(16)** *diplomatic* language is required here.

PR Managers like to call themselves 'Communications Managers,' to avoid being confused with 'Publicists and/or Marketers.' It is important to note that **(17)** *ethical* PR people do not like to be called 'Spin-doctors'. This is an over-used word and is especially associated with the media-machines of **(18)** *political* parties. Public Relations can mean many different things, which are entirely dependent on your point of view. **(19)** *Accreditation* is becoming more popular so that a particular skill-set can be identified, and ethical **(20)** *codes* of practice are being established. But, all in all, it's a wonderful and demanding **(21)** *profession*, and a very exciting and interesting industry in which to work.

Writing

The situation described in the letter below could turn out to be a Public Relations disaster for the famous London department store of Stairrods, especially because the author of the letter, Lord Henry, is very well known and he has lots of wealthy friends.

Calamity Castle,
Wenbridge,
Wenboroughshire, SE4 1XYZ
Phone/Fax 0129 002

Stairrods Ltd
Knightsbridge
London
W1

30 April, 2004

Dear Sirs

Hat Department order/delivery note 2517

With reference to the above order and delivery note, when I visited your store two weeks ago, I ordered seven Persian hats. The hats were to be delivered last Friday and left with my butler. (I was away in New York at the time and could not take delivery personally.)

Imagine my butler's surprise when he opened the large brown paper parcel to find not seven Persian hats, but seven Persian cats! Now, I like cats, but these animals are not very friendly and one of them scratched me rather badly when I went to give it some food.

Could you please let me know when you can collect the cats and deliver the hats. I must say, I require delivery rather urgently as my Turkish friends will be visiting me next week and they are allergic to cats.

I look forward to hearing from you.

Yours faithfully

Lord Henry de Bollingham-Smythe

A Write a letter of 120-140 words to Lord Henry apologising for the mistake and arrange to collect the cats as he requests. Remember to tell him when the hats will be delivered and suggest a way of compensating him for the trouble he has had — perhaps a box of chocolates might help? Use some of the words and phrases in the box below. Do not include addresses.

reference	apologies	a mistake by a new employee
error	assure you	will not happen again
telephone call	compensation	damages
valued business	your friends	doing business
forward	future requirements	do not hesitate
delivery		

Language Focus 1

Adverbs of Degree

In the Coursebook on page 82, four examples of adverbs of degree are given: *quite*, *rather*, *slightly* and *somewhat*. These adverbs are not generally used with verbs, but with adjectives or other adverbs.

Here is a point to remember about adverbs of degree. These adverbs are usually positioned directly in front of the adjectives or adverbs they describe.
*It was **rather** difficult to communicate due to cultural differences.*
*My business partner understands local customs **fairly** well.*

A **Use the words below to complete the following sentences.**

quite   rather   slightly
somewhat   very

1. Doing business across cultures can be a . . . . unpredictable affair.
2. Client needs are . . . . urgent in our organisation.
3. Our cost control has been . . . . better this year.
4. As our audience is international, it's . . . . important to use plain English.
5. Sticking to the agenda is . . . . a good idea.

B **Use the words below to complete the following sentences.**

really   pretty   fairly   far   nearly

1. The Marketing Department needs to come to a decision . . . . quickly.
2. It's a . . . . good idea to reinforce team spirit.
3. Tension at the meeting was . . . . strong, but we managed to diffuse it.
4. Pooling information makes things . . . . clearer for everybody.
5. Voicing disagreement to a client is . . . . always wrong.

C **Use the words below to complete the following sentences.**

entirely   equally   partly
perfectly   completely

1. Last year's market trends were . . . . predictable.
2. The British sense of humour is . . . . crazy.
3. The French and German quotations were . . . . competitive.
4. Direct translations are sometimes only . . . . correct.
5. To be . . . . honest, we must decide on our bottom line.

D **Use the words below to complete the following sentences.**

absolutely   much   exactly
distinctly   greatly

1. The negotiating skills of the Swedes are . . . . admired.
2. A friendly atmosphere is . . . . better for business.
3. They were . . . . embarrassed by the cultural misunderstanding.
4. Her advice on negotiating with the Korean company was . . . . right.
5. It is . . . . essential to offer a French buyer a vintage wine with his or her meal.

Language Focus 2

Whose language is it?

A Read the text below, which uses American English words, and fill in the substitutes, from the box below, which you would expect to hear used in the UK.

bonnet	sweets	petrol
hire-car	cupboard	holiday
tube	queuing	trousers
travelling case	biscuits	ground-floor
boot	chalet	porter
aerial	tap	return
waistcoat	puncture	nappy
motorway	director	

The **(1)** .... (vice-president) of a **(2)** .... (diaper) manufacturing company checked into a hotel on his way to a trade show. He was late because he had had **(3)** .... (a flat tire) on the **(4)** .... (freeway) and then he ran out of **(5)** .... (gas). He complained bitterly at the hotel because he had also damaged the **(6)** .... (hood), **(7)** .... (trunk) and **(8)** .... (antenna) of his **(9)** .... (rental car) when he tried to use the hotel garage. When the receptionist gave him his room key, he asked if she would book a **(10)** .... (round trip) ticket for him to Earl's Court exhibition halls. His room was on the **(11)** .... (first floor) and he asked the **(12)** .... (bell man) to leave his luggage next to the **(13)** . ... (closet) He went to take a quick shower, but the **(14)** .... (faucet) did not work properly. He was used to British hotels by now, though. From his **(15)** .... (suitcase) he selected a clean shirt, his favourite **(16)** .... (vest) and a comfortable pair of **(17)** .... (pants). The restaurant at the hotel was very busy so, as he hated **(18)** ...., (waiting in line) he decided to eat at a nearby café. Taking some of the complementary **(19)** .... (candy) and **(20)** .... (cookies) from the bedside table, he left his room, locking the door behind him. London was very busy, and after his meal, he took the **(21)** ...., (subway) which was overcrowded. All he could think of on his uncomfortable journey to the exhibition was his **(22)** .... (vacation) in three months time, in the family **(23)** .... (cabin) in Vermont.

Nationality and language

B Business is transacted across the world and business people meet colleagues from many different nations and cultures. Identify the nationalities and languages of the residents of the following capitals.

	nationality	language
a. Paris		
b. Copenhagen		
c. Beijing		
d. Ottawa		
e. Monaco		
f. Berne		
g. Ankara		
h. Seoul		
i. Beirut		
j. Cairo		
k. Amsterdam		
l. Canberra		
m. Jerusalem		
n. Wellington		
o. Dublin		

C Draw lines matching the festival to the country.

1. Japan	a. St Fermin
2. China	b. Ferragosto
3. France	c. New Year 22 March
4. Italy	d. Memorial Day
5. Switzerland	e. Thanksgiving
6. Mexico	f. Erschtä Auguscht
7. Belgium	g. Day of the Dead
8. Korea	h. Spring festival
9. The USA	i. Armistice Day
10. Spain	j. Clean Monday
11. Greece	k. Toussaint
12. Kazakhstan	l. Girls' Day

Language Development

(A) **Look at the minutes below from an international sales meeting. Which section A, B, C or D does each statement below refer to? You will need to use some letters more than once.**

A. A lively discussion took place between the French and German Sales Directors regarding the necessity of reporting market trends to their head office. It was agreed that exchanging information was vital to encourage good business relationships and to keep the company ahead of its competitors. Monsieur Martin favoured sending a written report to their head office every six months, but Herr Dr Splett thought the frequency should be every two months. The meeting participants generally agreed to a compromise of every quarter.

B. Señor Bilardi from Madrid proposed an in-depth analysis of client needs and a review of the company's technological lead. Herr Alpen from Zurich disagreed on some minor points, but accepted the necessity of some market research. He proposed increasing the advertising budget, but eventually struck a deal where the meeting participants accepted the Swedish proposal to commission some market research.

C. Herr Dahl from Copenhagen said, 'I am hoping to persuade the Board to allow us to give slightly larger discounts for bulk orders.' It was a point with which most people agreed. Monsieur Martin offered the opinion that profits should be ploughed back into R&D rather than giving them away to customers. Although there was general agreement on this point, it was decided not to come to a decision until the next meeting.

D. Some attention was given to the generation of new ideas and the pooling of information was raised once again. (See minutes of January 3rd.) Herr Dr Splett opposed benefits for staff as too expensive, but Mr Smith, the UK Sales Director, disagreed with him. However, a consensus was achieved when Monsieur Martin proposed the introduction of air-mile vouchers as a reward for employees who put forward suggestions which improved product design or operating efficiency.

··

1. The resolution to give price reductions was deferred until a later date.

2. Staff are to be given incentives if they introduce new ideas which benefit the company.

3. A market update has to be sent to headquarters every three months.

4. There was a disagreement between two delegates on a less serious matter.

5. An information flow was seen as essential to maintain competitiveness.

6. Consumer trends are to be examined in more detail.

7. The French representative wanted more money spent on R&D.

Writing

The Language of Diplomacy

A Re-write the letter below using diplomatic language from the Coursebook page 82 and the correct style for a business letter.

25 August 2005

Hi Guys

Thanks for your letter, but we didn't think much of your offer and we were a bit unhappy with it. We have been dissatisfied with your deliveries for some time and find the situation unacceptable. The bottom line is that you will have to improve your service if you want our business.

Where's the discount on the new lines you told us about, and what about the guarantees you promised? We were shocked about your expectations for us to arrange insurance costs, and, frankly, this is just not on. You are wrong about your product being unique; we can get quotations from the Far East any day. Anyway, we want a bigger rebate on the goods we have already received, because, frankly, what you are offering at the moment is just peanuts.

Sorry, but you obviously don't understand our needs. As we have to finalise the order in the next few days, we expect you to get back to us with some pretty appetising deals.

Regards

V. Nasty
Chief Buyer

The following fax was received in your office but, unfortunately, there was a fault on the line and the text does not have any punctuation.

B Re-write the fax, inserting punctuation as necessary.

FAX 25 January 2005

dear señor sastre thanks for your enquiry of 23 January for our superior model glue gun we can of course supply the number of units you asked for while adding your newly designed logo will cause a slight delay we do appreciate the urgency of your requirements our quality control department is aware of the current market trends towards higher safety awareness and client needs so we can assure you of our close attention to all your requests in this important area every effort will be made to deliver on time and in fact we shall use our express carrier service which guarantees next day delivery could you kindly let us know if you would like us to send a pro-forma invoice for which we would allow a discount of 5% provided payment is made within seven days otherwise we would be pleased to invoice you on normal monthly account terms which as you know allow only a 2½% discount for payment within 30 days as usual please do not hesitate to contact the undersigned if you require further information we look forward to receiving your valued orders in the future and assure you of our best attention at all times yours sincerely john cunningham area sales manager.

Global Advertising

Language Focus 1

Word order of adverbs

In the Coursebook on page 92, the Word Partnerships 5 section practices adverbs of degree, such as **widely** *regarded* and **clearly** *expressed*. The positioning of adverbs in sentences causes many difficulties, and care should be taken if you are translating into English directly from your mother tongue.

Some common mistakes are:
*I **last week** produced a report on our pricing policy.*
*The Marketing Manager likes **very much** the new advertising idea.*

Here are some basic rules for using adverbs correctly:

- Adverbs of degree are placed in front of an adjective or adverb.
  *She developed a **highly** cost-effective strategy.*

- Adverbs of frequency and manner are often placed between the subject and the verb.
  *They **often** fly British Airways because they like the tailfin logos.*
  *The new sales manager **quickly** identified the gap in the market.*

- Adverbial expressions of more than one word follow the verb and its object (if there is one).
  *Customers like our new global logo **very much**.*
  *Creative marketing increased our sales **quite a bit**.*

- Adverbs of desirability and presumption may be placed at the beginning of a sentence.
  ***Luckily,** our campaign was a success.*
  ***Obviously,** we can't over-spend our advertising budget.*

- Adverbs of time may come at the beginning or the end of a sentence.
  *Our advertisement was televised **last week**.*
  ***Next week**, the Andy Warhol exhibition opens at the National Gallery.*

A) Place the adverbs in the box between the subject and the verb.

| often usually only never always |

1. Saatchi and Saatchi make breathtaking ads.
   ....
2. Coca Cola uses a catchy jingle to advertise its products.
   ....
3. Nike employs a simple slogan to get its message across.
   ....
4. Consumers see what the ad agencies want them to see.
   ....
5. The company would consider a Benetton style campaign.
   ....

B) Place the adverbs/phrases in the box after the verb or its object.

| quite a bit   very much   at an astonishing rate   a lot   at seventy |

1. The MD finally decided to retire.
   ....
2. The market in developing countries grew.
   ....
3. Sales took off.
   ....
4. Controversial advertising doesn't appeal to the Chairman.
   ....
5. We use TV and radio advertising.
   ....

C) Place the adverbs/phrases in the box at the beginning or end of the sentences.

| fortunately   last year   next week (2)   clearly   on Tuesday |

1. Our advertising costs were covered by increased sales.
   ....
2. They asked us to send them their order.
   ....
3. We should receive the results of our market survey.
   ....
4. This change in market trends will require a new strategy.
   ....
5. The product range will be finalised.
   ....

Language Focus 2

In the article below about global marketing, most of the lines contain one word which is grammatically incorrect or does not fit in with the text. However some lines are correct.

A Read the article. Identify the incorrect word or write **CORRECT** at the end of the line.

Proof reading exercises, like this one, often cause students difficulties in exams. This is because, at a normal reading speed, your eye passes over text very quickly, causing you to miss the errors. In the article below, use your finger to carefully and slowly follow each line to find the error.

Examples:

0 Marketing used to be a relatively simple exercise based on deliberate what the ....*deliberate*....

1 professional marketers called, 'the four Ps': Price - Product - Place - Promotion. ...*correct*...

0	Marketing used to be a relatively simple exercise based on deliberate what the	....
1	professional marketers called, 'the four Ps': Price - Product - Place - Promotion.	....
2	The rapid growth of affordable Internet very connections has allowed the	....
3	remotest consumer to have instant access to the big most sophisticated of	....
4	products. Marketing is now a distinctly global activity and more Ps have been	....
5	added to the marketing mix: People – Packaging – Presence. World branding	....
6	now requires the huge amounts of money to be spent on TV advertising with	....
7	campaigns running simultaneously on many different countries. Market	....
8	segmentation is now much important and globalisation forces marketers to	....
9	concentrate on the common demands of international consumers. Advertisements	....
10	are made to appeal universally, although advertisements are been dubbed	....
11	into different languages to make each advertisement appear unique to a particular	....
12	market. However, there is a price to pay for the globalisation of marketing.	....
13	Products immediately identify for culture – for example, McDonald's is the	....
14	largest real estate owner in a world through its franchises, and it is the	....
15	personification of everything American. But when the World Trade Organisation	....
16	meet in Seattle in 1999, McDonald's was targeted by protestors, not because they	....
17	didn't like the hamburgers, but because they saw the company as an icon of the	....
18	unacceptable face of American globalisation.	....

Language Development

In the Coursebook page 91, the Word Partnerships 4 section practises using speech markers, such as *for example*, and *however,* to introduce new subjects or ideas. Markers help a speaker's presentation flow, and signal its direction and aims to the listener.

A **Read the presentation on creating a new logo for a global advertising campaign given by a Marketing Manager, and insert the correct *marker* from the list below.**

---

(1) ..., let me thank you all for coming to my presentation today. (2)... to start by talking about some of the great brands and logos which we all know so well – Nike's 'Just Do It', Apple's 'Think Different' and those great Budweiser frogs.

(3) ..., I'd like to get some ideas from you on how we should focus attention on our products in the global market place. (4) ..., are we going to come up with another Ronald McDonald – that was a real winner – or do we need a more user friendly, visually interesting image?

(5) ..., I'd like us to consider the advertising medium as an art form. (6) ..., look at the Andy Warhol tin of soup – if we could commission a work like that from an avant garde artist, who knows what our sales might achieve? I know the Finance Department would have something to say about that, so I'll leave that to the later part of my talk.

(7) ..., perhaps a jingle, or a whole song like the one Coke used in the '70s would be an ideal backing for our TV ads. (8) ... of pop songs going out of fashion very quickly, it may be the answer for us. (9) ..., we would have to watch the market very carefully and follow up with some strong market research to see if we were getting through.

(10) ... turn now to some of the breathtaking ads of Saatchi and Saatchi – do you remember the flying island of Manhattan? Now that was an advertising sensation. (11) ..., we could consider the minimalist approach to make our message compelling and memorable. Perhaps stunning images, a Beethoven sonata and a strong catch-phrase would do the trick? (12) ..., let me open the meeting so we can pool our ideas and come up with some original thoughts which let the world know we are the best in the business.

---

1. a. To begin with	b. For a start	c. Firstly
2. a. In the beginning	b. I'm going to	c. At the beginning
3. a. As well	b. Well	c. Also
4. a. Instantly	b. For instance	c. In an instant
5. a. In other words	b. In addition	c. After all
6. a. Eg	b. For example	c. Making an example
7. a. On another hand	b. On an other hand	c. On the other hand
8. a. In spite	b. Despite	c. Even though
9. a. In spite of	b. However	c. Despite
10. a. I want	b. Let me	c. I want that I
11. a. At last	b. Lastly	c. At least
12. a. Finally	b. At final	c. In the end

Writing

You have received the following e-mail from your agent in Hong Kong who has negotiated a deal with a Chinese exporter in Guangdong.

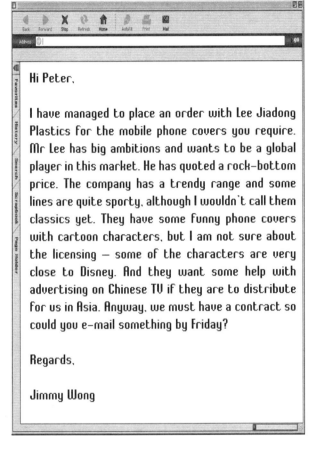

Hi Peter,

I have managed to place an order with Lee Jiadong Plastics for the mobile phone covers you require. Mr Lee has big ambitions and wants to be a global player in this market. He has quoted a rock-bottom price. The company has a trendy range and some lines are quite sporty, although I wouldn't call them classics yet. They have some funny phone covers with cartoon characters, but I am not sure about the licensing – some of the characters are very close to Disney. And they want some help with advertising on Chinese TV if they are to distribute for us in Asia. Anyway, we must have a contract so could you e-mail something by Friday?

Regards,

Jimmy Wong

Unfortunately, your company solicitor does not like using e-mail to send formal documents and he insists you write a letter to Mr Wong enclosing a standard company contract. He has left you the following note.

- How many phone covers can Lee supply a month?
- Is Lee going to go bust on us?
  (It happened before.)
- What's all this business about licensing?
- How much do they want to spend on TV ads?
- Do we need to establish a Letter of Credit?

A Write a letter of 120-140 words in a formal style, using some of the phrases below.

Dear Mr Wong

- Thank you for your e-mail nice to hear from you
- What volume of phone covers could you manufacture monthly?
- Is Lee financially sound you may remember a previous bankruptcy?
- We are nervous about placing a large order
- Have you checked credit rating?
- We are very interested in the humorous range
- Could you send samples?
- Would we need to apply for licences?
- We want to discuss distribution rights
- Is a Letter of Credit necessary?
- Who are Lee's bankers?
- A standard contract is enclosed
- Could you get Lee to sign and return?
- We look forward to hearing from you.

Yours sincerely
Encl: Standard form of contract.

Management Styles

Language Focus

Prepositions

Unit 8 of this book describes and practises prepositions connected to verbs. However, many prepositions are also used in relationship to nouns, noun phrases or equivalents, and adjectives.

Here are some basic points to remember about prepositions.

- They often connect a noun with another noun/ pronoun.
  What's **on** your mind?

- They also frequently connect a noun with an adjective.
  The Sales Manager was angry **about** the lost order.

- They are often used to describe time and place.
  time: after, during, for, in, since, before, at, till, about
  place: above, near, over, towards, through, under, on, off, down, up

A Connect the prepositions below to adjectives, nouns and noun phrases or equivalents in the sentences.

on	throughout	before	by	about

1. One in three new businesses is started up .... women.
2. Trainees require five years' field experience .... moving into management.
3. .... Tuesday, there is a forward planning meeting in the conference room.
4. Everyone was excited .... the change in management style.
5. .... the year, there are competitive exams for management positions.

B Use the prepositions of time below to complete the sentences.

about	at	since	during	for

1. She has worked as a director .... two years.
2. The new management team has been in place .... Christmas.
3. You will receive full pay .... the training period.
4. It can take .... four years to study for an MBA.
5. The Board meeting starts .... three o'clock on Wednesday.

C Use the prepositions of place below to complete the sentences.

above	across	inside	over	among

1. We have a number of female graduates .... our management trainees.
2. Managers need to practise their skills .... many disciplines.
3. In the past, women have found it difficult to rise .... the glass ceiling.
4. .... our organisation, promotion is on merit alone.
5. Ms Jacobs went .... to the Marketing Department last year.

D Use the prepositional phrases below to complete the sentences.

away from	far from
in front of	in the middle of
at the end of	

1. Head-hunters enticed our star manager .... us with a fat salary offer.
2. We were .... the Board meeting when the lay-offs were announced.
3. The candidates were .... perfect so we are going to re-advertise the post.
4. Ms Voss gets the key to the executive washroom .... June.
5. The car park is .... the new office complex.

E Add the missing prepositions to the sentences below.

1. The Human Resources Manager is . . . . holiday . . . . France
   for two weeks.

2. The new factory is . . . . a brownfield site . . . . the centre
   . . . . Manchester.

3. Recruit training has been delegated . . . . an agency.

4. Anita Roddick, head of Body Shop, went . . . . franchising.

5. We now do a lot of business . . . . developing countries.

6. Women are less ruthlessly individualistic . . . . their approach to business.

7. What is the stereotypical view . . . . a manager?

8. The HR Department deals . . . . promotion issues.

9. Our company deals . . . . precious metals, like gold and silver.

10. The company is owned . . . . the shareholders but controlled . . . .
    the managers.

F Add the missing prepositions.

1. Tight budgeting allowed us to offer the product . . . . £300 per tonne.

2. You can depend on our competitors . . . . offer a 10% discount
   . . . . the list price.

3. The share price has fallen . . . . 40% . . . . the last two years.

4. Our parent company informed us . . . . a price increase . . . .
   3% and 5%.

5. The Transport Manager made a saving . . . . maintenance
   costs . . . . 10%.

6. Payment is accepted . . . . cash or . . . . cheque.

7. The Sales Manager wants to try an offer of two . . . . the price
   . . . . one.

8. Could they send us samples . . . . express delivery . . . .
   their expense?

9. Our subsidiary company made a profit . . . . at least £1m . . . .
   that deal.

10. We can launch the company for an outlay . . . . $100,000.

G Add the missing prepositions.

1. She's extremely reliable and will be there . . . . time.

2. He has worked here full-time . . . . the last six weeks.

3. Their production staff were laid off . . . . two months.

4. Recruitment will increase . . . . the next year.

5. A new advertising executive will be appointed . . . . the beginning
   . . . . March.

6. Settlement . . . . full is due . . . . the end of thirty days.

Language Development

The article below asks the question,
'What is a manager?'

(A) **Read the article. For each question below, mark the letter a, b or c.**

The characteristics required by a good manager are well-documented and clearly definable. The person has to be, among other things, responsible, communicative, supportive and approachable. These adjectives are not gender-based, and focus attention on interpersonal skills, but a fierce debate still rages as to who make the best managers — men or women. The implication is that, providing an individual has all the right traits, he or she will automatically become a successful manager.

Surveys have been carried out to find out why certain individuals become national leaders. After all, if a person occupies the leading position in a country, there ought to be some common identifiable qualities which have universal appeal. The facts discovered are bizarre. For example, some leaders have been above average height or were well below it. They have been intelligent, but not geniuses and have had great enthusiasm, courage, determination, energy and faith. But possession of all these traits would be unusual in any one person. So these are necessary, but not sufficient conditions; good leaders have these qualities, but their possession alone does not make a good leader.

In his book, *Understanding Organisations*, Professor Charles Handy claims there is no right style of leadership. He says that leadership will be most effective when the requirements of the leader, the subordinates and the task fit together. This would seem to rather exclude personality from the equation. And yet, we can all recall managers whom we have liked or disliked, so there has to be more to the magic formula for a successful manager. Handy adds that managers need value systems which would acknowledge the desire for personal success and the planning and control of the actions of the people below them in the company hierarchy.

In his later theories, he defines managers as people who are responsible for making things happen. These are professionals who are accountable to the people who pay them and to the people working with and for them. Managers take responsibility for the actions of others. This is a popular modern definition of a manager, and while Handy accepts that personal characteristics like assertiveness, patience, loyalty and consistency are very important, he has added further vital statistics which he calls the four Ps: Projects (in which teams are involved), Professionalism, Passion and Pride.

1. In the first paragraph the writer says that managers:
a. can only be men.
b. need a balance of people skills.
c. are successful if they have strong, dominant personalities.

2. What does the writer believe makes a successful national leader?
a. people who are tall?
b. people who are intelligent and determined?
c. Research has been of little help.

3. Charles Handy thinks:
a. the tendency to be subordinate is vital for a manager.
b. managers should dominate the people below them.
c. there is no single form of good managership.

4. The modern definition of a manager is:
a. someone who is answerable to shareholders.
b. a person who is ambitious.
c. someone who has a duty to both his or her subordinates and superiors.

Writing

You have been asked by your Corporate Affairs Director to make hotel reservations for thirty people for a management conference during July or August. The following points are important.

The hotel must have a conference room with PowerPoint available.

All bedrooms must have private bathrooms.

The restaurant must be at least four-star, and there should be a swimming pool and gymnasium.

Your director has sent you the following hand-written note:

Please check if the hotel caters for handicapped people, as one delegate is in a wheelchair. And don't forget to ask for a good discount!

A **Read the advertisements, select the best hotel, and then write a letter of 120-140 words to the hotel management, attempting to obtain the best deal.**

- Royal Mariners Hotel Perth - A traditional enchanting hotel, all rooms en suite with TV/Telephone, tea and coffee. Three-star restaurant with mountain views. Conference room for 60 delegates with the latest computer facilities. Note - swimming pool closed for refurbishment during July and August.

The Rose Bower Hotel Plymton Set in three acres of rolling countryside, the perfect escape for a relaxing holiday. All rooms en suite with home comforts. Four-star award-winning restaurant with resident French chef. Visits to Exeter Cathedral and Dartmoor are a speciality. Bring the family. Please note, we do not offer conference bookings.

Hotel Bankside Bournemouth 120 en suite rooms and fully licensed bar. Twin, Double and Triple rooms available all year. Colour TV with 15 channels. Choice of 10 restaurants within walking distance. Parking for 80 cars. Sea views available. Four penthouse suites with magnificent sea views.

The Oliver Hotel Baston New, modern hotel close to motorway access. Perfect for the businessperson who needs conference facilities, Internet access and the latest software. All rooms en suite with tea, coffee and mini-bar. Five-star restaurant stays open until midnight. Shakespeare Bar with real ale. Superb Olympic-style swimming pool, sauna and gymnasium. We take pride in our ability to look after our wheelchair-bound customers.

THE OLD THATCHED BARN HAMLETON THE PERFECT COUNTRY HIDEAWAY—NO MOBILE PHONES, TVS OR COMPUTERS. THE PERFECT RETREAT FOR TIRED EXECUTIVES TRYING TO ESCAPE THE RAT RACE. FIVE-STAR RESTAURANT. SUPERB POOL AND GYMNASIUM TO BURN OFF THOSE EXTRA POUNDS. DISCOUNTS AVAILABLE FOR GROUP BOOKINGS.

Mergers and Acquisitions

Language Focus

Phrasal verbs

In the Coursebook on page 105 there is a quotation from Richard Branson where he says,
"… it's time **to break up** the company …"

To break up is a phrasal verb. This means that it is a compound verb comprised of a simple verb plus an adverb particle. The adverb particle looks like a preposition, but it does not show a relationship to the noun which follows or any other word in the sentence. It is linked to the verb itself.

Here are some points to remember about phrasal verbs.
- The simple verb and adverb particle are usually placed together in a sentence.
  She **heads up** the Finance Department.

- The simple verb and adverb particle can sometimes be separated by the direct object.
  It's time to **break** the company **up**.

- It is necessary to separate the simple verb and the adverb particle when the direct object is a pronoun.
  She heads **it** up.
  I need to call **him** in for a meeting.

- Most phrasal verbs can be replaced by single verbs of similar meaning.
  It's time to **fragmentise** the company.
  She **directs** the Finance Department.

A Replace the italicised verbs with phrasal verbs below.

> put in   put forward   put off
> put through   put back

1. The CEO will *propose* . . . . a hostile take-over bid at the meeting on Friday.
2. Trade barriers and tariffs have *postponed* . . . . the merger talks.
3. The riot in Seattle *delayed* . . . . the acquisition deal by three months.
4. The LBO was *initiated* . . . . by a firm of asset strippers.
5. Our brokers assured us the deal would be *completed* . . . . without a hitch.

B Replace the italicised verbs with the phrasal verbs below.

> break up   break away from   break into
> break off   break down

1. It was a mistake to *leave* . . . . our core business, we should have remained as we were and strengthened it.
2. A strategic alliance with the Japanese will help to *penetrate* . . . . the market.
3. Unless they accept our terms, we shall have to *cancel* . . . . the negotiations.
4. We can diversify into new markets more efficiently if we *split* . . . . the company.
5. Global media can be used to *reduce* . . . . consumer resistance.

C Replace the phrasal verbs with the correct forms of the verbs below.

> reclaim   demolish   admit
> employ   absorb

1. The new financial package will help us *take down* . . . . our competitors.
2. Human Resources will *take on* . . . . more staff during the transitional period.
3. The Greens want to *take back* . . . . the planet from the multi-nationals.
4. The WTO will not *take in* . . . . any new member countries this year.
5. AOL *takes up* . . . . advertising costs through its vast global network.

D Use your dictionary to find the different meanings of the following phrasal verbs.

take off . . . . look up . . . .

make up . . . . make out . . . .

get over . . . . run over . . . .

fall down . . . . put up . . . .

look into . . . . get on . . . .

run into . . . . fall out . . . .

take out . . . . look up to . . . .

switch off . . . . make over . . . .

get out of . . . . see out . . . .

E Insert the adverb particle to complete the phrasal verbs in the e-mail.

Hi Li-Ann

As you know, last month we took **(1)** . . . . three small companies in China. We have just about sewn **(2)** . . . . the local production of silk flowers and we should tie **(3)** . . . . the last few details next week. This will enable us to spread **(4)** . . . . into a larger market and to open **(5)** . . . . a whole new range of accounts when I come **(6)** . . . . to Hong Kong. I'm not so sure that I will have time to go **(7)** . . . . all the contracts, so could you please check them **(8)** . . . . for me? I tend to agree that you should take **(9)** . . . . an assistant as the work sure is building **(10)** . . . . I'm going to call in **(11)** . . . . a big trade show in Beijing— I only just found **(12)** . . . . about it. I have to drop **(13)** . . . . some samples to Harry Smith to see whether he could make **(14)** . . . . some of the floral displays at a more competitive price. See you when I get **(15)** . . . . the office next week.

Have a nice day.

Malcolm

Greenfield sites are pieces of land that have not previously been built on. Companies use these sites for new factories, very often collecting huge grants and tax breaks from governments keen to attract foreign investment and jobs.

F Draw lines to match the expressions using colours to their definitions.

1.	brownfield site	**a.** something useless
2.	white-collar worker	**b.** economic activities hidden from government taxes
3.	blue-collar worker	**c.** in writing
4.	black market	**d.** goods which may not be bought or sold
5.	white elephant	**e.** someone who works in an office
6.	in black and white	**f.** goods sold without the manufacturer's agreement
7.	black goods	**g.** domestic appliances – fridges and cookers
8.	white goods	**h.** illegal trade, usually for very high prices
9.	black economy	**i.** a manual worker
10.	grey market	**j.** an industrial area previously built on

Language Development

The extract below is from the annual report of a company chairman. It conveys a unique view of mergers and acquisitions.

A **Read the extract and choose the best word to fill each gap.**

Zedex's new organisational structure was implemented gradually during the year. The purpose of the new organisation is to **(1)** . . . . and give substance to Zedex's primary task: to support and serve its members, ie co-operative retail societies. At the time of writing my **(2)** . . . . , we currently have two million member households.

It is important to us to improve our business activities and to make them more **(3)** . . . . But it is also important to create conditions which encourage a more genuine and meaningful democratic participation of our elected representatives. There is no doubt in my mind that consumer co-ops have an important **(4)** . . . . to fulfil in today's and tomorrow's society. In an age when the **(5)** . . . . of maximum profit is preached and practised, the co-operative message of an economy **(6)** . . . . towards satisfying needs seems more urgent than ever before.

The tragic dilemma of the global community is the unjust **(7)** . . . . between the starving masses of the Third World and the **(8)** . . . . of the West. The gigantic problems created by this situation can hardly be settled by more **(9)** . . . . or protectionism. The solution lies in opting for a more co-operative alternative to open frontiers.

I am pleased to say that despite the 'greed is good' **(10)** . . . . of the global players, the interest in co-operative solutions is growing noticeably. The co-operative idea and form of **(11)** . . . . are seen by many young people as a solution to the problems created by the **(12)** . . . . market economy. I am proud to say that now that we are **(13)** . . . . our ladies' and menswear products in China, we are spending a considerable amount of money on the welfare **(14)** . . . . of the local workers. Similarly, we pay higher than average **(15)** . . . . rates in India to our manufacturers of Sport and Leisure goods. We look forward to another successful year of co-operation and profit for all.

1.	a. emphasise	b. stressed	c. mark
2.	a. letter	b. account	c. report
3.	a. active	b. efficient	c. potent
4.	a. mission	b. chore	c. object
5.	a. Bible	b. Koran	c. gospel
6.	a. pointed	b. adjusted	c. oriented
7.	a. gap	b. hole	c. width
8.	a. richness	b. affluence	c. wealthy
9.	a. capital	b. investing	c. capitalism
10.	a. moral	b. morale	c. maxim
11.	a. entrepreneur	b. enterprise	c. campaign
12.	a. liberal	b. open	c. free
13.	a. sourcing	b. discovering	c. starting
14.	a. benefits	b. hopeful	c. programme
15.	a. salary	b. fees	c. wage

Writing

You work in New York for a leading firm of Wall Street stock brokers which specialises in merger deals. You have just received the fax below from your London agent.

(A) **Look at the fax and the other information, on which you have also made some hand-written notes. Using all your hand-written notes, write a fax of 120 - 140 words to Peter Silversmith, a take-over specialist, advising him of the opportunity to make a quick raid on the shares.**

To: Wall Street Brokerage
From: Watson and Watson Acquisitions Ltd London
Subject: Take-over Opportunity

Date: 3 April 2005

Our analysis of the FTSE here in London has revealed that the directors of Tower Properties consider it is time to break up the company.

Action
- The directors have been involved in a sell-off of shares.
- The company's prime office block in Canary Wharf is up for sale.
- Black's Builders, the northern subsidiary company has already received bid offers.

Perfect time for takeover if we act immediately, I have alerted our brokers on the exchange floor

Tower Properties Share Prices Jan/Apr 2005

Jan: 230
Feb: 225

Shares expected to hold steady and
Mar: 200   *possibly rise if any bid rumours start*
Apr: 165

Rental income according to published accounts for latest three years

2002: £58m
2003: £120m
2004: £150m

Healthy rise in rents despite falling property values - they are ripe for a takeover, suggest you call me for urgent meeting

Tower Properties own three office blocks in the City, and two brownfield sites in the centre of Birmingham.

Mention these properties

Regards,
Mike Watson

13 UNIT — Business and the Environment

Language Focus

Conditional Sentences

In the article on managing the planet, a conditional sentence is used in the second paragraph to talk about the possibility of recycling waste products.

*For **even if** every household in the world recycled everything it used, solid waste **would be** reduced by a mere 2%.*

There are four categories of conditional sentences: the zero, first, second and third conditional. The sentence above uses the second conditional to express a hypothetical situation.

Here are some points to remember about conditional sentences.

Zero conditional
The *if* clause and the **result** clause are in the **present**.
It is used to express a universal truth that applies to the present.
*If you **heat** water to 100 degrees centigrade, it **boils**.*

First conditional
The *if* clause is in the **present**. The **result** clause is in the **future**.
It is used to express a possible outcome of a future possibility.
*If our industrial waste **causes** environmental damage, the company **will be** fined.*

Second conditional
The *if* clause is in the **past** (or the unreal past). The **result** clause uses a modal verb with an infinitive (without *to*).
It is used to express the possible outcome of a hypothetical situation, usually one that is unlikely.
*If I **won** the lottery, I **would buy** a villa in Spain.*

Third conditional
The *if* clause is in the **Past perfect.** The **result** clause uses a modal verb with the **Present perfect.**
It is used to discuss a past situation that is impossible to change. It is often used to express regret.
*If I **had known** it was your birthday, I **would have bought** you a present.*

A **Insert the verb in the correct tense to make zero conditionals.**

1. If tankers . . . . (spill) oil into the sea, they . . . . (destroy) marine life.
2. If carbon monoxide fumes from vehicles . . . ., (increase) air quality . . . . (decline)
3. If chemical effluent . . . . (flow) into our rivers, fish . . . . (die)
4. If the use of nuclear reactors . . . ., (spread) the danger of accidents . . . . (increase)
5. If we . . . . (use) biodegradable packaging, we . . . . (reduce) pollution.

B **Insert the verb in the correct tense to make first conditionals.**

1. If the greenhouse effect . . . ., (continue) the Polar ice cap . . . . (melt)
2. If industrial emissions . . . ., (not decrease) lung disease cases . . . . (rise)
3. If big corporations . . . . (keep on) polluting, who . . . . (control) them?
4. If we . . . . (carry on) producing acid rain, we (destroy) . . . . our forests.
5. If scientists . . . . (make) conservation profitable, industry . . . . (listen).

C **Insert the verb in the correct tense to make second conditionals.**

1. If companies . . . . (have) better incentives for recycling rubbish, they . . . . (be) more responsible.
2. If we . . . . (spend) more money on waste disposal, nature . . . . (be) safeguarded.
3. If polluters . . . . (pay) large fines, they . . . . (be) more careful about waste disposal.
4. If governments . . . . (be) really concerned about pollution, they . . . . (pass) tough laws.
5. If we . . . . (change) consumers hearts and minds, we . . . . (reduce) pollution.

D Insert the verb in the correct tense to make third conditionals.

1. If we . . . . (listen) to Greenpeace, we . . . . (have) a cleaner environment today.

2. If industrialists . . . . (invest) more money to solve pollution problems, they . . . . (have) more public sympathy today.

3. If oil companies . . . . (use) more modern tankers, there . . . . (be) fewer incidents of oil-covered beaches.

4. If corporate crime . . . . (be) cracked down upon in the 20th century, major toxic polluters . . . . (force) to pay for their irresponsible behaviour.

5. If the nuclear industry . . . . (be) more careful about waste discharge into the sea, our fish stocks . . . . (not deplete).

E Draw lines matching the words with words or phrases of a similar meaning.

1. toxic	a. power
2. consumption	b. science dealing with objects in movement
3. inequality	c. someone with privileged knowledge
4. antiquated	d. revival
5. dynamics	e. related to a corporation or group
6. corporate	f. poisonous
7. energy	g. imbalance
8. insider	h. out of date
9. restoration	i. depletion

F Read the memo and identify the types of conditional sentences by number. The first has been done for you.

From: Waste disposal department
To: All managers
Subject: Our increasing waste problem
CC: MD

Date: 6th August 2004

1. 2nd
2. . . . .
3. . . . .
4. . . . .
5. . . . .
6. . . . .
7. . . . .

(1) If we had infinite resources, we could invest in a furnace system to burn all the waste we generate. (2) Unfortunately, even if the shareholders paid for a unit, the local council would not let us use it. (3) If you light a fire anywhere these days, you get a fine! We have left waste disposal to solve itself for far too long. (4) The problem would have been avoided if we had put the 1990 inspector's report into action sooner. But investment in the environment was not a priority in those days. (5) If you ignore these things, you pay eventually. (6) If I had any ideas, I would bring them up at the next environmental meeting. (7) You will contact me immediately, I hope, if you have any flashes of genius.

Thanks

Heinrick

Language Development

Below is a proposal to install a new water treatment plant at
Lamb & Co Wool Washers Ltd.

A Match the headings to the correct sections in the proposal.

> other organisations involved   budget and backing
> description of activity   aims of project
> evaluation process

1 ....

To provide a new water treatment plant to control effluent discharge into the River
Nelland at Bostland from our wool washing factory at Briston.

2 ....

So that we can increase capacity at Briston, we intend to increase our current
discharge rate from one million gallons a day to two million. The processed water will
be up to drinking quality after passing through four filter beds. The liquid output will be
chemical free and will not cause damage to fish stocks in the river.

3 ....

£5 million investment capital to be set aside from profits for 2006, which will reduce
shareholder dividends.
The sum can be written-off against tax, and the local river authority has indicated its
willingness to give us a substantial grant.
The Department for the Environment also backs schemes like ours and the situation is
currently being investigated.

4 ....

A pilot project has already been in operation for the last year. Although the pumping
equipment has been run at half capacity, only minor problems were encountered.
Fortunately the breakdown, which took place in the second month of operation, was
not serious. But it did alert the engineers to the fact that a reserve lake was needed to
divert polluted water should the same thing happen when we are fully operational.

5 ....

A partnership has been formed with the Nelland River Authority and Briston Council.
It has been suggested we involve the local anglers to maximise public relations. All
publicity is good publicity and we may even get a mention on Anglia TV.

B Write true or false beside each of the following.

   a. The proposal is for a new plant at Briston. ....

   b. The company already discharges two million gallons of waste a day. ....

   c. The government will not tax the scheme. ....

   d. The pilot scheme showed the new arrangement would not need modification.

   ....

   e. Three groups are in the partnership, including local fishermen. ....

Writing

Your local council has written a letter to advise you of a new nuclear fuel reprocessing plant which is to be built on the edge of your town. You live in a particularly beautiful part of the country which has deserted beaches, rare birds and a rich and diverse environment for wildlife.

A **Read the letter and write to the council using 120-140 words. Do not include addresses. Mention the environmental issue to the council. Use your hand-written notes and add any extra points you see as relevant.**

New Factory for Our Town
5 June, 2004

Dear Mr Martindale

We are pleased to tell you that your council has granted a licence for Nukem and Zappem Ltd to build a nuclear fuel reprocessing plant on the outskirts of our town.

First I've heard about it - it's outrageous

We have very carefully evaluated any risks which might possibly be associated with the project, and we are pleased to tell you that, as far as we can see, there will be no danger to our residents. Nukem and Zappem Ltd have assured us that they will maintain the highest safety standards, in accordance with the industry regulations.

What about pollution - waste, radio-activity? Have they never heard of Chernobyl? Are they mad?

The project will mean work at last for some of our 2,000 unemployed coal miners who lost their jobs when the pits closed. And the local shopkeepers will benefit from increased trade, as the plant will employ 500 people in its first year.

I'm retired—I don't need a job. The plant will spoil my sea view.

Nukem and Zappem Ltd have promised to make arrangements to supply our town with cheap electricity and to allow local people to use the leisure facilities on their site.

Your council sees this as a step into the future for our town, and we hope you will continue to support your councillors in the next election.

You must be joking—I'm writing to my MP to protest!

Yours sincerely

John Bentley-Hook
Mayor

---

14 UNIT Finance and Credit

Language Focus 1

Going to and Will to express the future

Will is an auxiliary modal verb which is used with other verbs to express the future. *Going to* is a Present continuous tense also used to express the future.

Here are some points to remember about using *going to* and *will* to express the future.

- *Going to* is used when we think we know what is going to happen, or when we express something which we plan to do.
  I'm going to travel to New York on Friday.

- **Not** is placed before *going to* to express the negative.
  I'm not going to travel to New York on Friday.

- *Will* and its shortened form *'ll* are used to express a decision made at the moment of speaking. The negative form of *will* is *will not* or, in spoken English *won't*.
  We will have a party this afternoon to celebrate closing the deal.
  We'll ease the cash flow situation by calling in the debts.
  I won't agree to accept those terms.

- *Will* is also used to make offers and promises.
  I'll do it for you tomorrow. ***I'll*** put the cheque in the post.

- Both *going to* and *will* may be used for predictions, but *going to* is often used instead of *will* when we can see what is going to happen and the prediction is based on the present situation.
  The takeover was a mistake and we're ***going to lose*** *money.*
  The exhibition ***will last*** *for three days.*

A **Insert the correct form of *going to* or *will* or their negative forms.**

1. The Captain . . . . confirm the ETA Rotterdam this afternoon.
2. I . . . . pay this bill. They have overcharged for three items.
3. I . . . . discuss the cash flow problems with you later.
4. I . . . . ask the debt collector to pay a visit to the client.
5. It . . . . be difficult to explain the loss to the shareholders.
6. That company . . . . sit on invoices for two months before paying.
7. I . . . . need the lap top tomorrow, I . . . . use their mainframe computer.
8. I don't think they . . . . pay up front.
9. . . . . the buyer . . . . open a new Letter of Credit immediately?
10. Our competitors . . . . come to the conference – they have cancelled.
11. I . . . . arrange to send you a pro-forma invoice today.
12. . . . . you . . . . meet the client at his factory to inspect the damaged goods?
13. The Export Department . . . . send the licence next week.
14. . . . . you . . . . enter the purchases into the bought ledger?
15. Don't worry, I . . . . make the deadline.
16. This new product . . . . go like a bomb.
17. I heard that our rivals . . . . go bankrupt.
18. I . . . . pass this cheque for payment until I receive the credit note.
19. . . . . they order now or do they want to wait until next month?
20. We . . . . allow them to pay by cheque, it must be in cash.

Language Focus 2

A Read the following e-mail about some financial difficulties and replace the numbered expressions, pairing the adjectives in the box with the word *assets*.

fixed	intangible	wasting	net	liquid

Hi Jean-Pierre

Thanks for your last info. The financial situation is now desperate and creditors are knocking at our door. We have a certain amount of (1) . . . . (cash in reserve) in Euro Banque which is instantly accessible. Of course, our (2) . . . . (land, buildings and machines) can't be disposed of, even though they have increased in value recently. Our (3) . . . . (coal reserves) are now completely exhausted, but we still hold our diamond concessions in Angola. From a very quick audit, it looks as though the amount we have to pay to our creditors and for overdrafts – you might call these our liabilities – is greater than the (4) . . . . (total owed by our debtors, our cash in hand and our stock value). We have tried to value all the (5) . . . . (licences, patents and trade marks, even the goodwill), but we can't really turn these things into instant cash. I hate to admit it, but it looks like chapter eleven for us.

Regards

Marie-Claire

B Circle the correct words or phrases to complete the request for payment, which is written in a formal style.

Invoice 254   3 October 2004

Dear Señor Hernandez

Unfortunately we have not received payment of the above-mentioned invoice and the matter is now becoming (1) *urgent/crucial*. A further copy of our (2) *bill/statement* for August is (3) *enclosed/inside* with this letter. As agreed, we allowed you 30 days (4) *debit/credit* to help with your cash flow difficulties, but now we must (5) *insist/argue* payment is made without further (6) *hold ups/delay*.
Could you kindly (7) *remit/post* a cheque to reach us no later than Friday 15 October to clear your (8) *funds/account*. It is with regret that we must inform you that if we do not receive a (9) *bill/cheque* by this date we will have no (10) *alternative/difference* but to place the matter in the hands of our (11) *barrister/solicitors*.
In the meantime, further goods can only be supplied on a (12) *CWO/hire purchase* basis. We look forward to (13) *hear/hearing* from you.
Yours truly

A. Miser, Accountant

C Use your dictionary to explain the following:

to falsify	. . . .
to fiddle	. . . .
to garble	. . . .
to doctor	. . . .
sale goods	. . . .
seconds	. . . .
rejects	. . . .
bargains	. . . .
tribute	. . . .
bribe	. . . .
blackmail	. . . .
ransom	. . . .

Language Development

Ⓐ **Read the article on small businesses and credit regulation. For each statement below, mark the letter A, B, C or D of the paragraph it refers to. Some letters may be used more than once.**

A. Many small businesses experience difficulties with their larger customers because they do not have the muscle to put pressure on debtors. This has become a serious problem in recent years because governments are reluctant to regulate business-to-business relations. Bankruptcies are numerous in the small business sector of the economy because a demand for immediate payment often results in the cancellation of an order. Without the luxury of unlimited cashflow or capital reserves, small businesses suffer heavy casualties.

B. To minimise the risk of bad debt, careful credit checks have to be made into the financial standing of a customer. There are professional agencies who provide credit references worldwide, the most famous being Dun and Bradstreet. For small business owners, these checks are expensive and very often a banker's reference or a personal recommendation has to suffice. Very few businesses are in a position to insist on money in advance, and such requests for payment up front often result in damaged customer relations.

C. There are, however, ways around the problem of discouraging slow payers. The most obvious is to issue a pro-forma invoice which requires payment before goods are dispatched. Discount is usually offered because the customer is, in effect, paying in advance. A monthly settlement discount could be offered for payment within 30 days, which is the system used by most businesses in the U.K. Providing both sides play the game, cashflow is considerably eased for the small business while the customer benefits from cheaper goods.

D. For international trade, credit risk is minimised by using a Letter of Credit. This is established through a bank in favour of the supplier and payment is guaranteed providing the documents which accompany a shipment are presented in order. If the Letter of Credit is irrevocable, payment cannot be cancelled. Most small businesses would like to see the compulsory payment of interest on outstanding debts. A bad debt is, in effect, a free loan to the debtor. But governments have refused to introduce appropriate laws because of political sensitivity.

1. Banks can provide references which help small businesses.
2. There are a number of solutions to avoid maintaining debtors.
3. Cross-border trade is less risky with bank letters to guarantee payment.
4. Arranging for payment within one month is fairly common in the U.K.
5. Small businesses face a high risk of going bust.
6. Governments do not enforce interest payments.
7. Money does not flood into small businesses.

Writing

A Study the graph below and write beside the statements whether they are true or false.

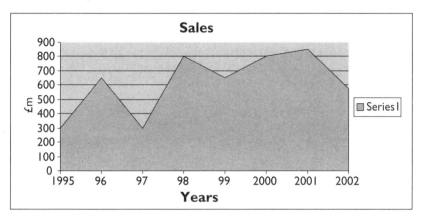

1. Sales started at £300 in 1995 . . . .
2. The graph flattened out in 1997 . . . .
3. Sales declined rapidly between 1996 and 1997 . . . .
4. The figures escalated sharply between 2001 and 2002 . . . .
5. Sales reached a peak in 2001 . . . .
6. Sales rose by more than 50% between 1995 and 1996 . . . .
7. In 1998, sales took a hike . . . .
8. Sales recovered between 1997 and 1998 . . . .
9. The year-end figure for 2001 was just below £600m . . . .
10. Sales rose marginally in 1999 . . . .

B Correct the statements about the graph below.

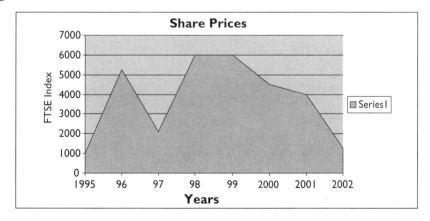

1. There was a sharply rise between 1995 and 1996 . . . .
2. Share prices levelled out in 1998 . . . .
3. In 2001, there was a dramatical decline . . . .
4. There was a raise in share prices in 1997 . . . .
5. Shares fell down from 4,500 to 4,000 in the year 2000 . . . .
6. There was a volatility period between 1996 and 1998 . . . .
7. Shares troughed between 1996 and 1998 . . . .
8. Shares made a sharp rocket in 1997 . . . .
9. The graph nosed dive in 2001 . . . .
10. Shares rose in value in 1995 . . . .

Economic Issues

Language Focus

The Passive Form

The passive form of the verb can be used with various tenses and it is useful to create an impersonal or formal style. It is often used in report and letter writing where the focus is on actions and results, not on the agent: an acting person or cause.

Here are some points to remember about the passive as compared to the active form.

Active
- The agent is the subject. It is placed before the result or object of the verb.
  Hyperinflation and soaring unemployment are causing the collapse of the world economy.

Passive
- The object of the verb is placed first and becomes the subject.
  The collapse of the world economy is being caused by hyperinflation and soaring unemployment.
- The agent is not usually mentioned in the passive unless it's unavoidable.
  The announcement was made at 3:00.
- When the agent is mentioned, the preposition by introduces it.
  The announcement was made at 3:00 **by** the MD.
- The agent is mentioned when the purpose and meaning of the sentence includes showing who or what the agent is.
  The role of Juliet was acted **by Lydia Schaffer.**
  The fire was caused **by negligence.**
- The passive is formed by combining the verb to be with the past participle.

Present simple
Thousands of jobs **are lost** every day due to the boom and bust cycle.
Past simple
Thousands of jobs **were lost** due to deflation.
Present continuous
Thousands of jobs **are being lost** because of speculative greed.
Past continuous
Thousands of jobs **were being destroyed** during the 1990s by merger mania.
Present perfect
Thousands of jobs **have been relocated** to take advantage of cheap labour.
Past perfect
Thousands of jobs **had been reduced** to the 'McJob' status.

A Rewrite the sentences using a passive construction. In some, you can choose not to mention the agent or cause.

1. Several factors cause an economic downturn.
   ....

2. Inflation caused worldwide misery and poverty.
   ....

3. Western companies are exploiting cheap labour in South East Asia.
   ....

4. The US government cuts unemployment benefit after six months.
   ....

5. In the past, low pay has created job dissatisfaction and labour troubles.
   ....

B Rewrite the sentences using a passive construction.

1. Too many imports and not enough exports widen the trade gap.

   ....

2. Bad labour relations did not attract foreign investors.

   ....

3. Inflation had pushed up prices 15%.

   ....

4. The company is reducing its investment programme.

   ....

5. The government figures predict a rise in population of at least 5%.

   ....

C Complete the business news article with the passive form of the verb in brackets.

The Grania corporation has announced that its main factory **(1)** ....
(relocate) to Mexico. Last year, in preparation for the move, three hundred
employees **(2)** .... (lay off) in the company's plant in the North East of
England. Following a unanimous vote at last month's Board meeting, it
(3) .... (decide) by the directors to issue redundancy notices to all
manual staff with effect from last week. Union representatives **(4)** ....
(advise) by their legal representatives and a strike vote **(5)** .... (consider)
by the workforce. The unions say the image of the North East **(6)** ....
(destroyed) by companies like Grania and the skill base will be lost forever.
An investment programme promised by the company, **(7)** .... (cancel)
and Grania **(8)** .... (blame) for pushing local unemployment rates up to
unacceptable levels. Public opinion is firmly behind the workforce and an open
meeting **(9)** .... (hold) at the civic centre tonight. Other unions
(10) .... (already/ask) to join in a show of solidarity with the Grania
workers and John Mahoney, the local MP **(11)** .... (expect) to chair the
meeting.

D Match the words with words or phrases of similar meaning.

1.	be sacked	a.	recession
2.	be made redundant	b.	corner the market
3.	deflation	c.	delay
4.	underclass	d.	take under state control
5.	immigrant	e.	be dismissed
6.	economical	f.	falling prices
7.	put off	g.	non-native
8.	nationalise	h.	underprivileged people
9.	slump	i.	something which saves money
10.	monopolise	j.	job loss due to over-manning

Language Development

A **Fill the gaps in the extract from a Bank of England fact sheet about monetary policy from the words below.**

One of the Bank of England's key responsibilities, as the **(1)** . . . . . bank of the UK, is the conduct of monetary policy. The Bank's **(2)** . . . . . is to deliver price stability (as defined by the Government's inflation target) by setting short-term interest **(3)** . . . . . The objective of monetary policy is **(4)** . . . . . stability – or, to put it another way, to restrain inflation or the general increase in the prices of **(5)** . . . . . or services. Uncertainty about inflation and future price levels is damaging to the proper functioning of the economy.

With a stable general price level, individual price **(6)** . . . . . can be read more clearly, and more rational decisions taken about whether to save or borrow, how much to invest and **(7)** . . . . . , and what and when to produce. In this way, price stability can help **(8)** . . . . . sustainable long-term economic growth.

Monetary policy operates by influencing the cost of money, ie the short-term **(9)** . . . . . of interest. The Bank sets an interest rate for its own **(10)** . . . . . with the market and that rate then affects the whole pattern of rates set by commercial banks for their **(11)** . . . . . and borrowers. This, in turn, will affect **(12)** . . . . . prices, eg shares and property, consumer and business demand, and, ultimately, output and **(13)** . . . . .

Broadly speaking, the objective is to keep aggregate demand as far as possible in line with the productive **(14)** . . . . . of the economy. If rates are set too low this may encourage inflationary pressures so that inflation is persistently above **(15)** . . . . . If they are set too high there is likely to be an unnecessary loss of output and employment, and inflation is likely to be persistently below target.

1.	a. middle	b. central	c. internal
2.	a. character	b. status	c. role
3.	a. payments	b. rates	c. duties
4.	a. price	b. cost	c. expenditure
5.	a. possessions	b. goods	c. belongings
6.	a. notices	b. signals	c. beacons
7.	a. consume	b. expend	c. deplete
8.	a. encouragement	b. forward	c. foster
9.	a. amount	b. rate	c. pace
10.	a. dealings	b. business	c. trade
11.	a. collectors	b. lenders	c. savers
12.	a. resource	b. asset	c. holdings
13.	a. job	b. work	c. employment
14.	a. volume	b. capacity	c. dimensions
15.	a. aim	b. objective	c. target

Writing

Your Board of Directors is going to discuss its investment policy for the next five years, following the national government elections which will take place in three months' time.

The party which is now in opposition is expected to be elected, and from the speech given by one of its members, it is clear that there will be some big changes in the new government's approach to business and enterprise.

 Write a report of 120-140 words, using the extract, to explain how these changes will affect your company.

Extract from a talk given by the Enterprise Party candidate at a meeting in the Swingate Centre, Winchester.

As you know, we have been in opposition now for ten years and the country is telling us it is time for change. When we were last in power, the GDP rose steadily from 1985 to 1995, but look what has happened under the current government. Not only has there been a decline in the figures, but a further fall is predicted for the next three years. We intend to reverse this trend by immediately reducing the burden on our wealth-creating businesses.

In addition we shall:
- cut income tax from the present iniquitous $22\frac{1}{2}$ % to 17%. This will immediately stimulate consumer demand and get the economy moving again.
- reduce the bank rate to those levels seen in the USA and Japan.
- give generous allowances and further tax breaks to companies who are prepared to invest in new projects.

The dramatic rise in unemployment will be tackled with subsidies for all new jobs created in our manufacturing industries. I honestly believe we have the means to get our economy moving again. The outlook for the next few years will only improve if you vote for the Enterprise Party. I utterly refuse to accept that the current government has the best policies; in fact they are strangling industry and handing our profits to our foreign competitors.

I know you may feel that politicians always promise the earth and will say anything to get themselves elected. But our party has commissioned leading economists to model the future of this country, and that future looks bright for all of us if we change our approach to encourage enterprise. More investment will be made in:
Railways—the whole system will be electrified and competitive rates will be offered for goods taken off the roads and sent by rail.
Infrastructure—more motorways will be built to ease road congestion, making it possible to reliably predict journey times.
Environment—your new government will fine any polluters heavily, and we promise to immediately make arrangements to clean up areas where standards have fallen below acceptable levels.

Please give us your support at the polls for a brighter and prosperous tomorrow.

Answer Key

Unit 1 Career Management

Page 6

A
1 Can, couldn't, can
2 shall be able to/can't
3 Shall Can
4 will be able
5 can't, can/can, can't
6 Can, can't
7 Will you be able, can
8 could, can't
9 Will/Won't we be able
10 Can, can

Page 7

A
1 was able to
2 could
3 was able to
4 were able to
5 could
6 was able to
7 were able to
8 could
9 was able to
10 were able to

B
1 was unable to
2 was unable to
3 couldn't
4 couldn't
5 was unable to/couldn't

C
1 could
2 couldn't
3 couldn't, could
4 could
5 couldn't
6 couldn't
7 could
8 could
9 Could, could
10 Could, couldn't

Page 8

A
1st row: 6, 1, 3
2nd row: 1, 2, 3 don't circle *managerial experience*
3rd row: 6, 2, 7; don't circle *marital status*
4th row: 4, 6; don't circle *sports team involvement*

Page 9

B
1 thoughtful
2 honest
3 generous
4 sociable/outgoing
5 sympathetic
6 patient
7 calm
8 cheerful
9 lively
10 independent
11 sensible
12 confident/calm
13 optimistic
14 hard-working
15 outgoing/sociable
16 reliable
17 responsible
18 kind
19 warm
20 efficient

Unit 2 Enterprise

Page 10

A
1 an, an
2 A, a
3 An, -
4 an
5 -, a
6 a, an
7 -
8 a
9 a
10 a, a

Page 11

A
1 The, the
2 The, -, -, -
3 The
4 the / -
5 The, the
6 -
7 the
8 the, -
9 the, the
10 The, the, the

B

1	A	5	the	9	the	13	the
2	-	6	The	10	the	14	-
3	-	7	-	11	the	15	the
4	the	8	the	12	the	16	the

Page 12

A
John: am going, this afternoon
Peter: Would go, am going to, right now
John: think, we will have to, is
Peter: would like, will be
John: don't worry, will fill (you) in, tomorrow

Page 13

B
The MD said the new model was ready. The PD said they could start the advertising campaign the following week. The MD said he would finalize the details the following day/on Thursday. The PD asked if the specification had changed from the previous week. The MD said it was the same as the one from three weeks before. The PD promised to get the hard copy for the following week.

Unit 3 E-business

Page 14

A
1 Do you deal in ....?
2 Is Martha Lane ...?
3 Did he lose money ....?
4 Do you do ....?
5 Does the company ...?
6 Did she register ...?

B
1 You are frequently on the Net, aren't you?
2 You are a computer genius, aren't you?
3 You are computer literate, aren't you?
4 The dotcom phenomenon is over, isn't it?
5 Elise never banks online, does she?
6 The Internet can't replace life, can it?

C (suggested answers – there may other possible answers)
1 What does IT mean?
2 How far is it …?
3 How much does it weigh?
4 When did the market …?
5 What did he say?
6 Whose wife is called …?
7 Why don't you like …?
8 How long have you worked …?
9 Where did you find …?
10 Why do you like …?

Page 15

A
1	b	6	c	11	b	16	b
2	a	7	a	12	b	17	c
3	b	8	b	13	b	18	a
4	c	9	c	14	c	19	a
5	b	10	a	15	c	20	c

Page 16

A
1	a	4	b	7	e	10	i
2	j	5	k	8	d	11	h
3	f	6	c	9	g	12	l

Unit 4 Brand Management

Page 18

A
1	come	6	is
2	prosecute	7	sells
3	are	8	live
4	wants, comes	9	hold/holds
5	has	10	remains

B
1	are generating	6	are taking
2	is handling	7	are they still pouring
3	is living	8	is increasing
4	are making	9	are not giving in
5	are soaring, are going	10	is making

Page 19

C
1	achieved	6	went
2	took over	7	dived
3	introduced	8	shot down
4	had	9	trickled in
5	played	10	was, quoted

D
1	are	12	is
2	have	13	is thinking
3	are making	14	is suffering
4	grow	15	need
5	are eating	16	makes
6	is investigating	17	is going
7	succeeds	18	shoot down
8	is going	19	is going
9	needs	20	realise
10	seems	21	is happening
11	is building		

Page 20

A
1	c	6	b	11	b	16	a
2	b	7	b	12	c	17	c
3	c	8	a	13	b	18	c
4	c	9	c	14	a	19	a
5	a	10	c	15	c	20	c

Page 21

A
1 Right hand address not aligned left
2 Left hand address has commas
3 Post code missing
4 Date written out
5 Dear Sir or Madam
6 Wud-would
7 Lik-like
8 Oner-owner
9 Supper-super
10 Roadster-full stop required
11 frends-friends
12 modle-model
13 metalic-metallic
14 hurry; comma required
15 ofer-offer
16 twenti-twenty
17 ordres-orders
18 recieved-received
19 befor-before
20 midnite-midnight
21 friday-Friday
22 repli-reply
23 cuopon-coupon
24 envalope-envelope
25 benifit-benefit
26 unrepeatible-unrepeatable
27 Rememember- Remember-comma missing
28 won-one
29 mis-miss
30 Truly yours-Yours faithfully
31 sells-Sales
32 manger-Manager
33 s.p.-P.S.
34 why-Why
35 aks-ask
36 drove-drive
37 conveneince-convenience-fullstop missing

Unit 5 Prices and Commodities

Page 22

A
1	Since	7	because
2	because	8	Since
3	Since	9	Because
4	because	10	As
5	As	11	because
6	Since		

B
1 As
2 Since
3 As
4 Since
5 Since

Page 23

A
1 steady
2 strongly
3 slight
4 sharply
5 marginally
6 slowly
7 small
8 dramatically
9 steadily
10 rapidly

Page 24

A
1 e
2 f
3 i
4 g
5 b
6 a
7 c
8 d
9 h

B
1 value
2 priceless
3 valueless
4 forgery
5 fraud
6 counterfeit
7 worth
8 invaluable
9 valuable

Page 25

A
1 FOB
2 FOR
3 CIF
4 CANDF
5 FRANCO
6 Pro-Forma

Unit 6 Corporate Entertaining

Page 26

A
1 Wash
2 Crisp
3 cut
4 Shake
5 place
6 Peel
7 slice
8 Mix
9 Chop
10 add
11 Sprinkle
12 Put
13 pour
14 Season
15 Toss
16 enjoy
[Answers may vary]

Page 27

B
1 Open
2 Close
3 make
4 Pass
5 hand
6 Have
7 Get
8 order
9 ask
10 call, book

C
1 Let's
2 Let's not
3 Let's
4 Let's
5 Let's not
6 Let's
7 Let's
8 Let's not, Let's
9 Let's
10 Let's

D
1 Take
2 fill
3 bring
4 Pour
5 Bring
6 tip
7 add
8 Remember
9 Pour
10 leave
11 Brew
12 pour
13 Spoon
14 add

E Go/turn/Walk on/take/cross/Keep/turn/follow/Go through/Give/Have

Page 28

B
1 f
2 h
3 e
4 a
5 b
6 d
7 c
8 g
9 j
10 i

Page 29

A
1 e
2 c
3 a
4 g

B
1 b
2 d
3 e
4 f

Unit 7 Innovation

Page 30

A
1 has advised
2 have fluctuated
3 has just failed
4 has run out
5 has been

B
1 has the project cost
2 Have you (ever) visited
3 Has the boss agreed
4 have they killed off
5 Has he chosen

C
1 haven't signed
2 have not seen
3 hasn't redesigned
4 has not made
5 hasn't made

Page 31

A Students' own answers

Page 32

A
1 a
2 b
3 b
4 b

Page 33

A
we are doing business
we need to make
we must avoid
we have made progress
by spending a lot of money
if you need to make
showed that we are not

making a big effort
can be discussed
to make a phone call
to do a good job
by helping you

Unit 8 Public Relations

Page 34

A
1	in	4	through	7	to	10	on
2	by	5	for	8	to/with		
3	to	6	for	9	with		

B
1	to	4	of	7	with	10	with
2	by	5	into	8	at		
3	to	6	by	9	on		

C
1	about/of	5	of	9	of
2	with	6	by	10	to
3	on	7	of		
4	with	8	to		

Page 35

A
1	d	6	c	11	c	16	c
2	b	7	d	12	d	17	a
3	c	8	a	13	a	18	b
4	c	9	b	14	c	19	a
5	c	10	d	15	c	20	b

Page 36

A
1	description	12	concept
2	appraises	13	offices
3	association	14	occasion
4	approval	15	area
5	conversation	16	tactful
6	newspapers and TV	17	moral
7	workers	18	governmental
8	processes	19	certification
9	spread	20	principles
10	statements	21	occupation
11	pamphlets		

Unit 9 Cultural Awareness
Page 38

A
1	somewhat	4	rather
2	very	5	quite
3	slightly		

B
1	fairly	4	far
2	really	5	nearly
3	pretty		

C
1	entirely	4	partly
2	completely	5	perfectly
3	equally		

D
1	much	4	exactly
2	distinctly	5	absolutely
3	greatly		

Page 39

A
1	director	13	cupboard
2	nappy	14	tap
3	puncture	15	travelling case
4	motorway	16	waistcoat
5	petrol	17	trousers
6	bonnet	18	queuing
7	boot	19	sweets
8	aerial	20	biscuits
9	hire-car	21	tube
10	return	22	holiday
11	ground-floor	23	chalet
12	porter		

B
a	French/French	l	Australian/English
b	Dane/Danish	m	Israeli/Hebrew
c	Chinese/Chinese	n	New Zealander/ English
d	Canadian/English	o	Irish/English/Irish
e	Monegasque/French		
f	Swiss/German/French/ Italian/Romansch		
g	Turkish/Turkish		
h	Korean/Korean		
i	Lebanese/Arabic		
j	Egyptian/Arabic		
k	Dutch/Dutch		

C
a	Spain	g	Mexico
b	Italy	h	China
c	Kazakhstan	i	Belgium
d	South Korea/ The USA	j	Greece
e	The USA	k	France
f	Switzerland	l	Japan

Page 40

A
1	C	5	A
2	D	6	B
3	A	7	C
4	B		

Unit 10 Global Advertising
Page 41

B Dear Señor Sastre

Thanks for your enquiry of 23 January for our superior model glue gun. We can, of course, supply the number of units you asked for. While adding your newly designed logo will cause a slight delay, we do appreciate the urgency of your requiremnets.

Our quality control department is aware of the the current market trends towards higher safety awareness and client needs, so we can assure you of our close attention to all your requests in this important area. Every effort will be made to deliver on time and, in fact, we shall use our express carrier service which guarantees next day delivery.

Could you kindly let us know if you would like us to send a pro-forma invoice for which we would allow a discount of 5%, provided payment is made within seven days. Otherwise, we would be pleased to invoice you on normal monthly account terms, which, as you know, allow only a $2^1/2$% discount for payment within 30 days .

As usual, please do not hesitate to contact the undersigned if you require further information.

We look forward to receiving your valued orders in the future and assure you of our best attention at all times.

Yours sincerely

John Cunningham
Area Sales manager

Page 42

A
1. always make
2. Coca Cola often/usually uses
3. Nike usually/often employs
4. Consumers only see
5. The company would never consider

B
1. retire at seventy
2. grew quite a bit
3. sales took off at an astonishing rate
4. the chairman very much
5. advertising a lot

C
1. Last year, our
2. order on Tuesday.
3. survey next week.
4. Clearly, this change
5. 'Fortunately, the product range will be finalised next week'.

Page 43

A
1	correct	8	much	15	correct
2	very	9	correct	16	meet
3	big	10	been	17	correct
4	correct	11	correct	18	correct
5	correct	12	correct		
6	the	13	for		
7	on	14	a		

Page 44

A
1	c	5	b	9	b
2	b	6	b	10	b
3	c	7	c	11	b
4	b	8	a	12	a

Unit 11 Management Styles
Page 46

A
1	by	4	about
2	before	5	Throughout
3	On		

B
1	for	4	about
2	since	5	at
3	during		

C
1	among	4	inside
2	across	5	over
3	above		

D
1	away from	4	at the end of
2	in the middle of	5	in front of
3	far from		

Page 47

E
1	on, in	5	with	9	in
2	on, in, of	6	in	10	by, by
3	to	7	of		
4	into	8	with		

F
1	at	8	by, at
2	to, off	9	of, on
3	by, during	10	of
4	of, of between		(answers may vary)
5	on, of		
6	in, by		
7	for, of		

G
1	on	5	by, of
2	for	6	in, at
3	for		
4	during		

Page 48

A
1 b   3 c
2 b   4 c

Unit 12 Mergers and Acquisitions
Page 50

A
1 propose/put forward
2 postponed/put off
3 delayed/put back
4 initiated/put in
5 completed/put through

B
1 leave/break away from
2 penetrate/break into
3 cancel/break off
4 split/break up
5 reduce/break down

C
1 take down/demolish
2 take on/employ
3 take back/reclaim
4 take in/admit
5 takes up/absorbs

D [students will have differing answers]

Page 51

E
1 over
2 up
3 up
4 out
5 up
6 back
7 over
8 out
9 on
10 up
11 at
12 out
13 off
14 up
15 into

F
1 j
2 e
3 i
4 h
5 a
6 c
7 d
8 g
9 b
10 f

Page 52

A
1 a
2 c
3 b
4 a
5 c
6 c
7 a
8 b
9 c
10 c
11 b
12 c
13 a
14 c
15 c

Unit 13 Business and the Environment
Page 54

A
1 spill, destroy
2 increase, declines
3 flows, die
4 spreads, increases
5 use, reduce

B
1 continues, will melt
2 don't decrease, will rise
3 keep on, will control
4 carry on, will destroy
5 make, will listen

C
1 had, would be
2 spent, would be
3 paid, would be
4 were, would pass
5 changed, would reduce

Page 55

D
1 had listened, would have had
2 had invested, would have had
3 had used, would have been
4 had been, would have been forced
5 had been, would not have been depleted

E
1 f
2 i
3 g
4 h
5 b
6 e
7 a
8 c
9 d

F
1 2nd
2 2nd
3 0
4 3rd
5 0
6 2nd
7 1st

Page 56

A
1 description of activity
2 aims of project
3 budget and backing
4 evaluation process
5 other organisations involved

B
A false
B false
C true
D false
E false

Unit 14 Finance and Credit
Page 58

A
1 will
2 I'm not going to
3 'll
4 will
5 It's going to be
6 will
7 I won't, 'll
8 will
9 Is the buyer going to
10 aren't going to
11 'll
12 Are you going to
13 is going to
14 Are you going to
15 'll
16 is going to
17 are going to
18 I won't
19 Will
20 We won't

Page 59

A
1. liquid assets
2. fixed assets
3. wasting assets
4. net assets
5. intangible assets

B
1. urgent
2. statement
3. enclosed
4. credit
5. insist
6. delay
7. remit
8. account
9. cheque
10. alternative
11. solicitors
12. CWO
13. hearing

C Students' own answers

Page 60

A
1. B
2. C
3. D
4. C
5. A
6. D
7. A

Page 61

A Graph 1
1. false
2. false
3. true
4. false
5. true
6. true
7. false
8. true
9. false
10. true

B Graph 2
1. sharp rise
2. flattened out
3. dramatic decline
4. rise in share prices
5. shares fell from
6. a period of volatility
7. there was a trough in share prices between…
8. shares rocketed in 1997
9. nose dived
10. rose

Unit 15 Economic issues

Page 62

A
1. The economic downturn was caused by several factors.
2. Worldwide misery and poverty were caused by inflation.
3. Cheap labour in South East Asia is being exploited by Western companies.
4. Unemployment benefit is cut after six months./ Unemployment benefit is cut after six months by the US government.
5. In the past, job dissatisfaction and labour troubles have been created by low pay.

Page 63

B
1. The trade gap is widened by too many imports and not enough exports.
2. Foreign investors were not attracted by bad labour relations.
3. Prices had been pushed up 15%./ Prices had been pushed up 15% by inflation.
4. The investment programme is being reduced./ The investment programme is being reduced by the company.
5. A rise in population of at least 5 % is predicted./ A rise in population of at least 5% is being predicted by government figures.

C
1. is being relocated
2. were laid off
3. had been decided/was decided
4. are being advised
5. is being considered
6. is being destroyed
7. had been
8. is being blamed
9. is being held
10. have already been asked
11. is expected

cancelled/was cancelled

D
1. e
2. j
3. f
4. h
5. g
6. i
7. c
8. d
9. a
10. b

Page 64

A
1. b
2. c
3. b
4. a
5. b
6. b
7. a
8. c
9. b
10. a
11. c
12. b
13. c
14. b
15. c

Model Answers

Unit 2 Enterprise Page 13   Letter

5 April 2005

Dear Sirs

New Electronic Circuit

I would like to offer you a new electronic circuit which I have recently invented. I have been interested in electronics since I was at school, and, in fact, I won an Electronic Engineering prize when I was only 15 years old.

I am sure my product will offer great advantages to the mobile phone industry and I am looking for a company like yours which might wish to invest in my revolutionary design.

I have consulted the Business Advisory group and they believe my project will be successful, but we have to act quickly because no other company has this product on the market. I have enclosed my business plan for your information and I would appreciate your comments.

I do hope we able to work together on this exciting development, and I look forward to hearing from you.

Yours faithfully
John Smith.
Encl: Business Plan

Unit 3 E-business Page 17  Report

April 6 2005

Car hire for visit to France

Proceedings: Several French websites and three of the main UK car-hire companies were checked to find the most competitive rates.
Findings:
- All the UK car companies offer Mercedes C Class vehicles, but the rates were too expensive. The French companies also hire Mercs and the cheapest, BagnolesRus, have an E-class at 400€ per week as a special offer. This is, unfortunately, over our budget at the moment.

- Reliablerunners, another French company, do not operate at Nantes airport, although they have a taxi service to their nearby offices and they refund the fare. Air conditioned vehicles are available from 280€ which is well within our budget.

Recommendations: There are some very cheap offers, but, as we have to consider reliability and our image with the client, the best company seems to be Reliablerunners.

Margarita Cassel
Transport Manager

Unit 6 Corporate Entertaining Page 29   Memo

To: Fadime
I want to arrange something different for our next client entertainment event on 3rd August. As we are inviting families this year, I suggest number one on the list – the go-carts and jeeps look great fun..
S.H.

Unit 7 Innovation Page 33 B Letter

28 September 2005

Dear Mr Loony

Underwater TV Set

Thank you for your letter of 21st September regarding your new invention.
Unfortunately, due to difficulties with suppliers and intense foreign competition, we no longer manufacture electrical items. Although we have discussed the potential of your product, we feel that there would not be a large enough market to justify going into production.

We would also like to point out that companies like ours would only consider products where we have exclusive rights of manufacture. Because of the high costs involved, most people in our industry try to avoid licensing agreements.

Our Managing Director will be away on a tour of the Far East for the next three months. He has requested that no appointments are made until he returns, so, regrettably, we are unable to offer you an appointment at present.

Thank you for your interest in our company.

Yours sincerely
Peter Finch
New Products Division

Unit 8 Public Relations Page 37 Letter

2 May 2004

Dear Lord Henry

Hat Dept Order/Delivery Note 2517

Thank you for your letter of 30 April with reference to the above mentioned delivery note. We would like to offer you our sincere apologies for our error which was caused by a mistake at our warehouse by a new employee.

We have revised our procedures and would like to assure you this situation will not happen again. We have arranged to deliver your hats next Friday and we shall telephone you before delivery. At the same time, we shall collect the cats.

By way of compensation, and further apology, we would like to offer you a box of our *Supreme Speciality Chocolates From All Over The World*, specially selected from our food hall.

We can assure you we highly value your business and we look forward to supplying your future requirements. Please do not hesitate to contact us if you have any further problems.

Yours sincerely
Angela Rogers
Dispatch department.

Unit 9 Cultural Awareness Page 41 Letter

28 August 2005

Dear Peter,

Quotation

Thank you for your offer but, unfortunately, we would be unable to accept it. I'm sure I don't need to remind that your deliveries have been falling below your contractual obligations in recent months. I sincerely hope you are able to improve the situation so that we may continue doing business together.

I was very surprised that you expect us to arrange insurance costs as this has not previously been part of our agreement. Actually, we were hoping for a slightly more substantial rebate from you. We are currently looking at several quotations from your competitors, although we would, of course, be very reluctant to change suppliers.

As we would like to place our order within the next few days, could you possibly re-submit your offer on a more competitive basis. I look forward to hearing from you.

Yours sincerely
Hiroko Satsuma

Unit 10 Global Advertising Page 45 Letter

June 2 2005

Dear Jimmy

Phone Cover Contract

Thank you for your e-mail regarding Jiadong Plastics. We would like to go ahead, but the legal department have asked me to clarify one or two points.

This company went bankrupt two years ago and we need some evidence to show they are now financially sound. Could you please check their credit rating and report back as soon as possible? We like the cartoon range but we would like samples and an idea of the volume they could supply.

If we need to establish a Letter of Credit, we will use City Bank as usual, but we need to know the name of Lee's bankers. Licences are no problem and we will handle the applications from this end. Distribution rights need further discussion and a contract is enclosed for Lee's signature.

We look forward to hearing from you.

Yours sincerely,
Peter Paterson

Unit 11 Management Styles Page 49 Letter

4 February 2005

Dear Sirs

Conference Booking

I noticed your advertisement for the Oliver Hotel in Leisure Magazine and I would like to make a reservation for a conference.

Your advertisement mentions that you have Internet access, but could you please confirm that PowerPoint is available? Also, we have one employee who uses a wheelchair – could you please confirm you cater adequately for wheelchairs with easy access ramps and lifts.

We are expecting thirty delegates to attend and single rooms would be preferred, but perhaps you could let us know your suggested accommodation arrangements. The conference will take place over three days during July or August, depending on the dates you have available.

We look forward to receiving your best quotation, including group booking discount, as soon as possible.

Yours faithfully
Ms Rosita Hernandez
Entertainment Manager

Unit 12 Mergers and Acquisitions Page 53 Fax

3 April 2005

Dear Peter

Tower Properties Opportunity

A merger opportunity has arisen here in the City, but we shall have to act quickly. There are plenty of rumours suggesting Tower Properties are ready to break up the company.

They are selling a major London property, and there were reports in yesterday's Financial Times that directors are disposing of shares. A bid has already been made for one of Tower's northern subsidiaries, although the deal has not yet been finalised.

Shares have fallen since January, but the current interest may start a rally. Tower own three properties in the City and some brownfield sites in Birmingham. Although the value of commercial property is falling, rents are still going up, so it looks like you need to start moving on the shares as soon as possible.

Please call me to arrange a meeting.
Regards
Nicola Holickson

Unit 13 Business and Environment Page 57 Letter

6 June 2004

Dear Sirs

Proposed Nuclear Reprocessing Plant

Thank you for your letter of 5 June regarding the above mentioned new factory. I was unaware of the council's plan and I am very worried about the situation.

Nuclear reprocessing involves the discharge and disposal of highly poisonous waste, such as radio-active particles, which build up to dangerous levels in our environment. And accidents will happen – do I need to remind you of the disaster at Chernobyl?

We have beautiful surroundings here with unpolluted beaches, migrant sea birds and rare flowers. Are you prepared to endanger all of this for short term economic gains? I retired here three years ago and I bought my house for its sea view – which your new factory will completely ruin.

I am writing in protest to my Member of Parliament and will do everything possible to stop this crazy scheme from going ahead.

Yours faithfully
J. Martindale

Unit 15 Economic Issues Page 65 Report

Investment Policy for Immediate Future

Proceedings: I attended the meeting of the Enterprise Party candidate at the Swingate centre Winchester on Friday 2 October 2004.

Findings: It looks as though the new government, if elected, will be much more helpful to business than the current one. The most interesting points which affect our future development are:
A reduction in income taxes.
Lower bank rates.
Encouragement for new capital investment.
Subsidies for manufacturing jobs.

Promises were also made to tackle the problems on the railways and roads, especially the motorways, and fines will be introduced for polluters (we have problems at the Raston plant)

Recommendations: I suggest, without hesitation, we increase our donations to the Enterprise Party to help fund their election campaign.

Mary Alexander
Corporate Affairs Director 3 October 2004

The Cambridge Business English Certificates Vantage Examination

If you are using this book to help you with your studies for the examination, the comments in the boxes below show you in detail why this letter would pass with the highest band five mark.

See unit 2 page 13

---

5 August 2005 | date

Dear Sirs | correct greeting to a company, no comma

New Electronic Circuit | heading

I would like to offer you a new electronic circuit which I have recently invented. I have been interested in electronics since I was at school, and, in fact, I won an Electronic Engineering prize when I was only 15 years old.

'I would like' - use of polite form of a modal verb. Natural language used.
First bulleted point mentioned.

I am sure my product will offer great advantages to the mobile phone industry and I am looking for a company like yours which might wish to invest in my revolutionary design.

Second bulleted point mentioned, but expressed in candidate's own words, not copied from the question. Good structure and vocabulary.

I *have* consulted the Business Advisory group and they believe my project will be successful, but we have to act quickly because no *others* company has this product on the market. I have enclosed my business plan for your information and I would appreciate your comments.

Other bulleted points covered, summarised and expressed in the candidate's own words.
Formal language used throughout - 'I have consulted.'
Effectively organised with appropriate use of cohesive devices 'but we have...' Error -*others*- not serious.

I do hope we able to work together on this exciting development, and I look forward to hearing from you.

Standard ending and correct use of "I look forward to."

Yours faithfully

John Smith | Correct salutation and name given, no comma.

Encl: Business Plan | Enclosure noted.

Look at the question in this book on page 13:

- All points have been included and summarised in the candidate's own words as far as possible.

- The one small error - *others* - is minimal and would not lose marks.

- The letter has a positive effect on the reader.

- 140 words are used, excluding headings. Candidates will be allowed a small number of extra words, but should try to stay within the limit set.

Test of Writing

For BEC Vantage, candidates are required to produce two pieces of writing:

- an internal company communication; this means a piece of communication with a colleague or colleagues within the company on a business-related matter, and the delivery medium may be a note, message, memo or e-mail;

- and one of the following:

  - a piece of business correspondence; this means correspondence with somebody outside the company (e.g. a customer or supplier) on a business-related matter, and the delivery medium may be letter, fax or e-mail.

  - a report; this means the presentation of information in relation to a specific issue or events. The report will contain an introduction, main body of findings and conclusion; it is possible that the delivery medium may be a memo or an e-mail.

  - a proposal; this has a similar format to a report, but unlike the report, the focus of the proposal is on the future, with the main focus being on recommendations for discussion; it is possible that the delivery medium may be a memo or an e-mail.

Part One

In this part candidates are presented with the context in the task rubric. This explains the role the candidate must take in order to write a note, message, memo or e-mail of around 40 to 50 words using a written prompt. It also identifies who the message is to be written to. The prompt is included in the instructions, in the form of bullet points clearly stating the pieces of information that must be incorporated into the answer.

Where the delivery medium specified for a Part One answer is a memo or an e-mail, candidates need not include to/from/date/subject details.

Here are some examples of questions for Part One:

1. You are the Human Resources manager for a large cash and carry wine store.

   Write a **memo** to all staff explaining your boss' instructions:

   - Your car park is being repaired and space is limited for customer and staff parking.
   - Employees have been using your Managing Director's personal parking space and he is unable to park his car conveniently.
   - He has asked you to write a memo to all staff pointing out, tactfully, that cars must be correctly parked only in the designated areas.

   Write 40 - 50 words.

   Write on the opposite page.

2. You are travelling to Boston USA to meet a client, and you will first be meeting your American agent.

   Write an **e-mail** to her organising the meeting:

   - Your date and expected time of arrival in Boston.
   - Your flight number.
   - Request a booking for a double hotel room as your wife is travelling with you.

   Write 40 - 50 words.

   Write on the opposite page.

Part Two

In the second Writing task, candidates are required to write 120 to 140 words in the form of business correspondence, a short report or proposal. There is an explanation of the task and one or more texts as input material. These texts may contain visual or graphic material and have, 'handwritten' notes on them.

There is no significant difference between the format required for proposals and reports. At this level, reports must be clearly organised and should not contain letter features. There is no particular requirement for subheadings, particularly given the length of the report.

Where the delivery medium specified for a Part Two answer is a letter, candidates need not include postal addresses in their answer. Similarly, where the delivery medium specified is a fax, candidates need not include 'fax header' details, and where the delivery medium specified is a memo or an e-mail, candidates need not include to/from/date/subject details.

An example of a Part Two question is shown on page 80.

Test of reading
Part One

This is a matching task. There are four short texts on a related theme (e.g. descriptions of a group of products, or advertisements for jobs) or a single text divided into four sections. Although the context of each text will be similar, there will also be information that is particular to each text. The texts are labelled A - D. Candidates are presented with a set of seven items which are statements related to the texts. They are expected to match each statement with the relevant text.
See Unit 6 page 28, Unit 9 page 40, Unit 14 page 60.

Part Two

This is a matching task, comprising a text that has had six sentences removed from it and a set of seven sentences labelled A - G. Candidates are required to match each gap with the sentence which they think fits in terms of meaning and structure. The first gap is always given as an example so that candidates have five gaps left to complete. When they have finished this part there will be one sentence left which they have not used.
See Unit 3 page 16, Unit 10 page 44.

Part Three

This task consists of a text accompanied by four-option multiple choice items. The stem of a multiple choice item may take the form of a question or an incomplete sentence. There are six items, which are placed after the text. Sources of original texts may be the general and business press, company literature and books on topics such as management. Texts may be edited, but the source is authentic.
See unit 7 page 32, Unit 11 page 48.

Part Four

This is a multiple choice cloze test with fifteen gaps, most of which test lexical items, and may focus on correct word choice, lexical collocations and fixed phrases. The texts chosen for this part will come from varied sources but they will all have a straightforward message or meaning, so that candidates are being tested on vocabulary and not on their comprehension of the passage.

See Unit 4 page 20, Unit 12 page 52, Unit 15 page 64.

Part Five

In this task, candidates identify words that have been introduced into a text in error. This exercise can be related to the authentic task of checking a text for errors, and suitable text types therefore include letters, publicity materials, etc. The text contains twelve numbered lines, which are the test items. Further lines at the end may complete the text, but these are not test items.

See Unit 10 page 43.

Some general advice for candidates

Reading Section

- This section takes one hour, and contains five tasks, allowing roughly ten minutes per question with ten minutes to check your work at the end of the exam.
- Work carefully through the wide range of topics in the course book to broaden your knowledge of business related matters. The exercises in this workbook will help you to familiarise yourself with the style of the exam questions.
- Read the business sections of newspapers, magazines dedicated to business topics, catalogues and company reports to broaden your business English vocabulary.
- Make sure you are familiar with the language required to describe graphs, data and measurements.
- In parts 1, 2, and 3 of the exam, read through the text and the suggested answers, before making a choice.
- Fill in your answer sheet in a **soft medium pencil** and take **a rubber** into the exam so that you will be able to make any necessary alterations.

Writing Section

- This section takes 45 minutes, and contains two tasks. The second task will take longer to complete, so apportion your time carefully.
- Write your answers clearly and legibly in **ink** on the answer sheet provided.
- English or American spellings may be used.
- Use synonyms for words in the question wherever you can, adding adjectives and adverbs. Avoid copying out sections of the question into your answer.
- Read all the question rubrics twice before writing anything. Check and highlight any, 'handwritten' notes in the text of the cue material because if you miss any items in your answer, you will lose marks. Always check your written work.
- The Language Focus sections of this workbook will help you to reach the required level of grammar to pass the Written Section of the BEC Vantage exam.

And finally – Good Luck!

Sample Paper

PART TWO

- You work for BusinessSpace plc, a company which rents fully serviced offices to other businesses. You have just received the fax below.

- Look at the fax and the other information below, on which you have already made some handwritten notes.

- Then, using **all** your handwritten notes, write a **fax** in reply to Reinhard Mieter.

- **Write 120 – 140 words.**

- Write on the opposite page.

FAX

TO: BusinessSpace
FROM: Reinhard Mieter
SUBJECT: **Renting Office Space**

Further to our discussion last week we have now decided to rent office space from you for the next twelve months:

Requirements

- one office of 10 m², two of 15 m², one of 20 m²
- must be on same floor
- 40 parking spaces

Please confirm if this office space is vacant in Central Tower.

offer 10% discount for 18-month booking

four left, different floors, no parking – suggest Opera Place

CENTRAL TOWER (CT)	
Offices currently vacant	Size m²
CT 19	10
CT 24	20
CT 53	15
CT 54	15

OPERA PLACE (OP)	
Offices currently vacant	Size m²
OP 34	10
OP 39	20
OP 46	10
OP 47	15
OP 48	20
OP 49	15

OPERA PLACE

Why choose Opera Place?

- 300 parking spaces
- good public transport connections
- wonderful views

mention these benefits

four same floor